Drawing Fashion

Bill Thames

Instructor, Design Department
Fashion Institute of Design
and Merchandising
San Francisco, California

GLENCOE

Macmillan/McGraw-Hill

New York, New York
Columbus, Ohio
Mission Hills, California
Peoria, Illinois

Cover Illustration: Bill Thames

The author would like to thank the following
people who generously lent original artwork for
giving him permission to reproduce it:

James Galanos, p. viii
Jeanne-Marc, p. viii
Bill Blass, p. ix
Diane Von Furstenberg, p. ix
Liz Claiborne, p. ix
Patti Baker, p. 116
Aubrey Wilson, p. 116
Phoebe Evans, p. 117
Mary Cheung, p. 117
Dorian Leong, p. 117

Library of Congress Cataloging in Publication Data

Thames, Bill.
  Drawing fashion.

  Includes index.
  1. Fashion drawing.   I. Title.
TT509.T49   1984   741.67′2   84-23377
ISBN 0-07-063722-9
ISBN 0-07-063724-5 (TRADE ED.)

Send all inquiries to:
GLENCOE DIVISION
Macmillan/McGraw-Hill
15319 Chatsworth Street
P.O. Box 9609
Mission Hills, California 91346-9609

ISBN 0-07-063722-9
ISBN 0-07-063724-5 {TRADE ED.}

Printed in the United States of America.

5 6 7 8 9 10 11 12 13 14 15   AGK   00 99 98 97 96 95 94 93

Contents

1 Drawing the Figure 1

2 Drawing the Garments 55

3 Rendering the Fabrics 119

Preface

Drawing Fashion aims to help people in the fashion business to develop a valuable communications tool. For fashion illustrators, conveying images in visual form is obviously a necessary professional skill. For the fashion designer, a drawing is the best way to describe a garment concept. For others employed in fashion-related positions, the usefulness of drawing is less apparent, but it is nevertheless an important asset. People engaged in the manufacture of textiles and apparel, buyers for retail stores, small fashion shop owners, and even consumers can all benefit from learning how to read, interpret, and utilize fashion drawing.

A fashion drawing of a garment is styled so that it is immediately recognized as *fashion* and not merely as drawing. The emphasis is on the garment. Appeal and excitement must be conveyed. The technique may range from the most impressionistic "mood" drawing of an editorial illustration or couture designer concept to flat, working sketches displaying with accuracy all the garment's details.

The purpose of this book is to help the student in the classroom or the experienced professional in the design room to develop and improve his or her fashion drawing skills. The method explained in this book can also encourage a young person about to make a career choice, and it can be used for entertainment by people of all ages who enjoy fashion.

The "Bill Thames Method"

Drawing Fashion is the result of my years of experience as a free-lance illustrator and as a teacher. The step-by-step procedure presented here is one that I developed, after analyzing my own approach to the fashion figure. Its benefits are twofold: It helps me to control proportions when I draw figures of many sizes, and it provides a formula for the students to *plan* their figures, encouraging the people who were convinced they couldn't draw.

The double-page spreads contain a sequence of numbered steps for the student to follow. Directions are offered to correspond with each number, and each step is color-coded to keep the sequence in view. Each spread is a complete lesson ending with a finished example. This is to avoid confusing and time-consuming page turning.

For teachers who wish to use *Drawing Fashion* as a textbook, a teacher's manual is available. It provides suggestions for presenting the sequence and process approach within a classroom setting.

Organization

The text is organized into three parts, corresponding to the three components of a fashion drawing: the figure, the garment, and the fabric. Each part has its own color for quick access. For the best results, each part should be practiced in sequence. This order of presentation parallels the way a fashion drawing develops, first sketching the figure's stance, then drawing the garment on the figure, and finally rendering the characteristic qualities of the fabric.

As the student studies and practices each part in succession, his or her skills will grow to the point of being able to approach the more difficult requirements of the next part. Part One, Drawing the Figure, offers my very simple formula for controlling the proportions of the current fashion figure. This formula, given on page 8, will work no matter what size drawing is required. Part One explains the proportions of the male fashion figure as well as the female and describes the changing proportions of children's figures from toddlers to adolescents. The student is also introduced to stances, volume, faces, hair, hands, and feet.

The importance of silhouette is described in Part Two, Drawing the Garments. This part employs step-by-step techniques for the drawing of a selection of basic garments. The skills acquired by doing these exercises until the results are satisfactory can then be applied to more complex designs. To enlarge the students' fashion perspective, a gallery of twentieth-century classics (and some curiosities) concludes this part.

Part Three, Rendering the Fabrics, begins with a section in which each double-page spread shows three steps to full color. Part Three then discusses fabric weight and body and demonstrates how to control the scaling of patterns and textures. Step-by-step instructions for the rendering of key fabrics are provided. Part Three concludes with a description of presentation skills and portfolio preparation.

Acknowledgments

I wish to thank Frederick Bennett of The Fashion Institute of Technology, New York City, for his painstaking review of several drafts of this book and for his many insightful suggestions. His kindness in interrupting his vacation to visit with me and "talk shop" was greatly appreciated. I also owe a debt of gratitude to Dennis Brozynski and Sharon Moran of the International Academy of Merchandising and Design, Chicago. They reviewed the entire book and offered many helpful suggestions. I also want to acknowledge the help of the following friends and associates over the many years this book has been "in the works": Betty Bachrach, Peter Barrett, Eva Bortnick, Lee Brady, Sam Douglas, Mike Drum, Mark Hendricksen, Richard Ingersoll, Grace Ma, Ellen Murphy, Tim Sheehy, Susan Turbin, and Tom Turbin.

Most of all, I am grateful to my students—for whom this book was written.

Bill Thames

Gallery of Fashion Designer Drawings

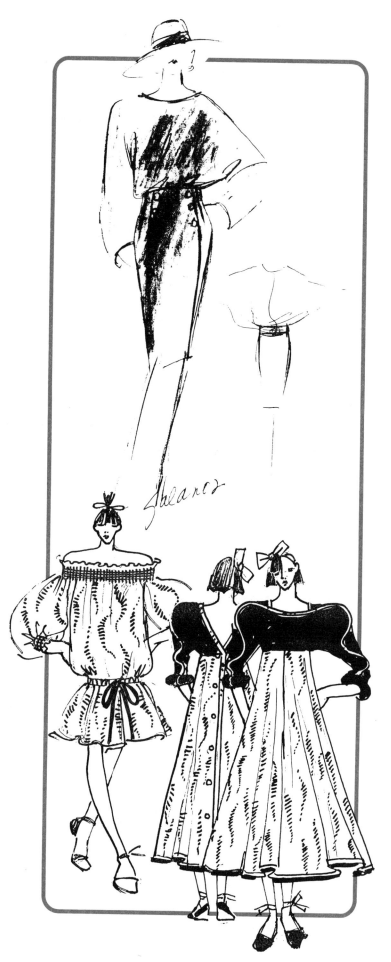

Fashion design drawings range from very flat working sketches to highly rendered full-color illustrations that often become very valid artistic statements. In the middle are the drawings that run the gamut from primitive to quite sophisticated. The mastering of one pose or a small group of poses can suffice as long as they convey silhouette, proportion, and instructions to assistants and sample makers. For the public and the press, the services of a professional illustrator can be obtained.

Theatrical costume designs require the most complete rendering. They must show not only every last sequin, bangle, or trim, but must also suggest and flatter the features of the star for whom they have been created.

Though drawing is only one of the many skills involved in fashion design, most designers who do not draw or do not draw as well as they would like almost inevitably regret this lack, no matter how successful they are otherwise.

The drawings shown here are reproduced with permission from these talented designers:

p. viii (*top*)—James Galanos
   (*bottom*)—Marc Grant for Jean-Marc
p. ix (*left*)—Bill Blass
       —Bill Blass couture sketches
  (*center*)—Diane Von Furstenberg
   (*right*)—Liz Claiborne

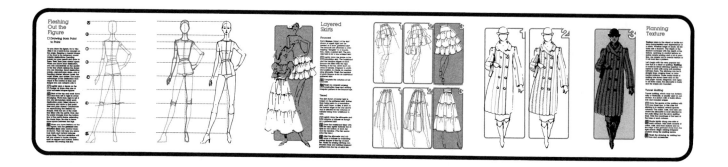

How to Use This Book

This volume contains a thorough guide to drawing fashion for both the student and the working designer. It also offers a strong foundation for the fledgling fashion illustrator.

The ability to present design concepts in a visual form is one of the designer's most important tools. Describing a garment verbally will create as many images as the designer has listeners; whereas, an accurate drawing of the garment will communicate one image to all. Designer drawings can range all the way from flat, working sketches to elaborate, full-color renderings. The latter technique is especially necessary for theatrical costume design.

Fashion illustrations are different from designer's drawings. In fashion illustration, the garment exists not just as a concept, but as a product. This product must be reproduced in a current, flattering manner that emphasizes its most important fashion features.

When drawing fashion, the student is confronted by three familiar components: the human body, the garment, and the fabrics from which the garments are crafted. The student's task is to stylize these three into a current fashion drawing. For the designer this is an early step in a process that will result in a finished garment. For the illustrator, however, the drawing is the finished product and art school training is strongly recommended.

Since both designers and illustrators of fashion are constantly beset by irrevocable deadlines, this book was written with one eye on the clock. Emphasis is placed on practice as the only way to develop the skill to work swiftly. Sequence of approach and process is employed to obtain maximum results as quickly as possible. There are no magic substitutes for hard work, but a number of time-saving devices are included to aid the student in presenting concepts swiftly, accurately, and with as much fashion flair as possi-

ble. Throughout, the student is encouraged to increase her or his judgment and to develop a personal style.

The exercises in this book are arranged on double page spreads to keep the entire process in view when in use. Emphasis is placed on color-coded "sequence and process" as drawing aids and time-saving devices. Each exercise will lead the student step-by-step, visually and verbally, to the completion of a number of well-proportioned fashion figures in desirable poses. Practice each exercise until the final drawing can be accomplished accurately and with comparative ease. When you are in the planning stages of a drawing, always use a pencil. Later you can switch to pen or marker.

As each figure is completed, pin the drawing to the wall or prop up your pad and step back at least four feet. At this new distance look for any miscalculations or irregularities. You've used the rules, now trust your eye and develop your judgment. Don't be easily discouraged. Professionals often draw a number of drafts until they produce one that they will accept. Many of your early attempts will go wrong. When this occurs, refer closely to the directions and diagrams to discover the source of the difficulty. Keep repeating the exercise until the problem is identified and solved. With determined practice and perseverance, a variety of fashion figures should be readily at your command.

The process described in *Drawing Fashion*, the "Bill Thames Method," is not the only approach to drawing fashion—but it is a simple and effective process that works.

Educate yourself. Acquire some heroes among the fine fashion designers and illustrators of past and present. Collect and copy your favorites and allow them to influence you. Soon enough your personal taste and style will develop. Your drawings will then be clearly your own.

Part One
Drawing the Figure

For the designer, the most basic of the current fashion poses work best. Illustrators often take a freer approach to stance and pose, always taking care, however, to flatter the garments they are drawing. Both designers and illustrators should choose poses which emphasize important design elements. The object is to strongly depict the fashion look but never to obscure or distort a garment's design.

The female fashion figure now in favor is slender, leggy, and lithe. The male figure is more muscular than the female, with an athletic appearance. The hands and feet of both males and females are boldly scaled—an open hand will cover the face. The top half of the fashion figure consists of the head, neck, and torso. The bottom half is legs.

For the designer, faces, hairstyles, and accessories are only used to express a total concept. The illustrator relies heavily on them to impart a look of current fashion. In the windows of better stores, you will find excellent examples of overall fashion presentation. The mannequins in these displays are created and dressed by experts, with appropriate accessories, stances, and hairstyles. They exist only to show clothes as smartly as possible, as does the drawn fashion figure.

For the sake of clarity, the figure drawings that soon follow have been kept simple. You may feel your first efforts to reproduce them lack fashion verve. Don't be put off. First master the basic techniques presented. Then you can inject your own interpretation of fashion flair.

Basic Tools and Materials

All you need to start are a pad of paper, some sharp pencils, and an eraser. Here is a list of supplies for a beginner:

- 11" × 18" or 14" × 17" news-print pad (inexpensive paper, for early exercises).
- 11" × 18" or 14" × 17" layout bond pad (better-quality white paper, for more finished work).
- A dozen soft-lead drafting pencils such as Eagle 314s.
- Kneaded erasers. (These erasers don't leave crumbs and will not tear paper; however, they will not erase heavy, labored lines. Clean them by kneading them with your fingers.)
- Drawing board with tilt support. (This support can range from four bricks propping a board, to tabletop tilt mechanisms, to actual drafting tables.)
- Felt-tip pens, with both fine and medium points.
- Roll of masking tape, push-pins, pencil sharpener, container for pencils and pens, tray for organizing materials.

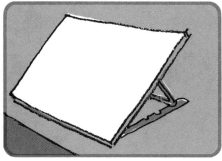
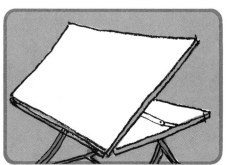

Drawing Board Posture and Organization

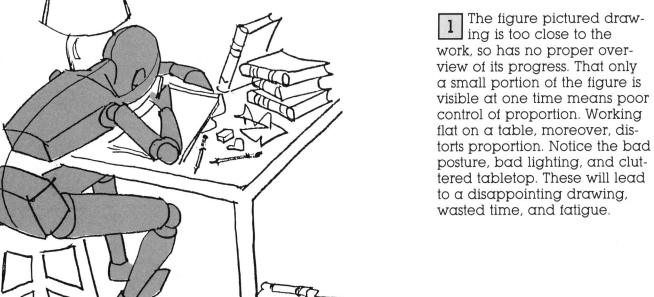

1 The figure pictured drawing is too close to the work, so has no proper overview of its progress. That only a small portion of the figure is visible at one time means poor control of proportion. Working flat on a table, moreover, distorts proportion. Notice the bad posture, bad lighting, and cluttered tabletop. These will lead to a disappointing drawing, wasted time, and fatigue.

2 Here, the figure pictured sits up with a view of the whole drawing as well as the source material (the open book). Working on a tilted drawing board under good light that shines directly on the work from above will result in better control of the drawing. Notice the handy wastebasket and the well-organized supplies on a tray within easy reach. All these pluses will contribute to rewarding results.

Placement on the Page

The shape of your paper is called the **format**. Whatever your format, place the figure on the page so that the top margin is smaller than the bottom margin.

1. Too-large figure runs off page.
2. Too-small figure tucked into corner.
3. Too-low figure shortened in attempt to fit it all in.
4. Correctly placed figure working well within its format, using conventional margins.

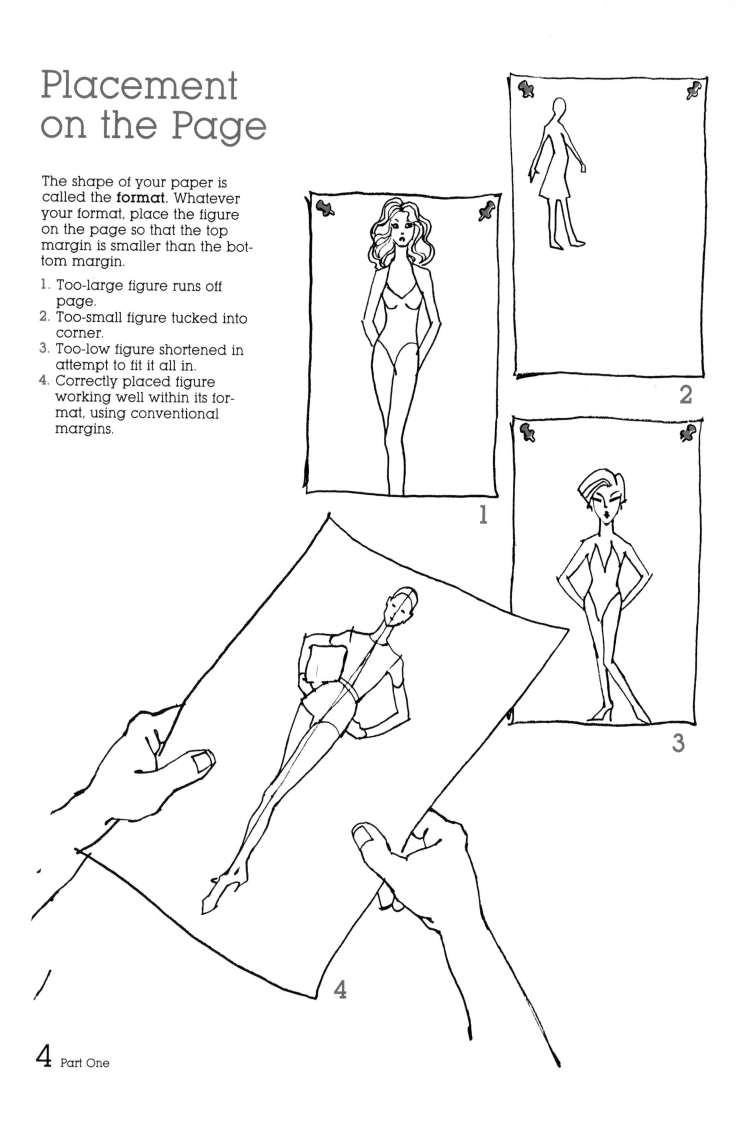

Scaling the Figure to the Page

No matter the size of the paper, the figure should be **scaled** to fit it. Plan a figure that fills the page, as shown on the facing page. The various parts of the body are drawn in **proportion** to each other at the scale you have chosen. Proportion has to do with the relationship of figure parts to each other and to the whole figure. **Scale** has to do with the ratio of adjustment chosen. On page 8 is a formula which will give you control in scaling the figure to the page.

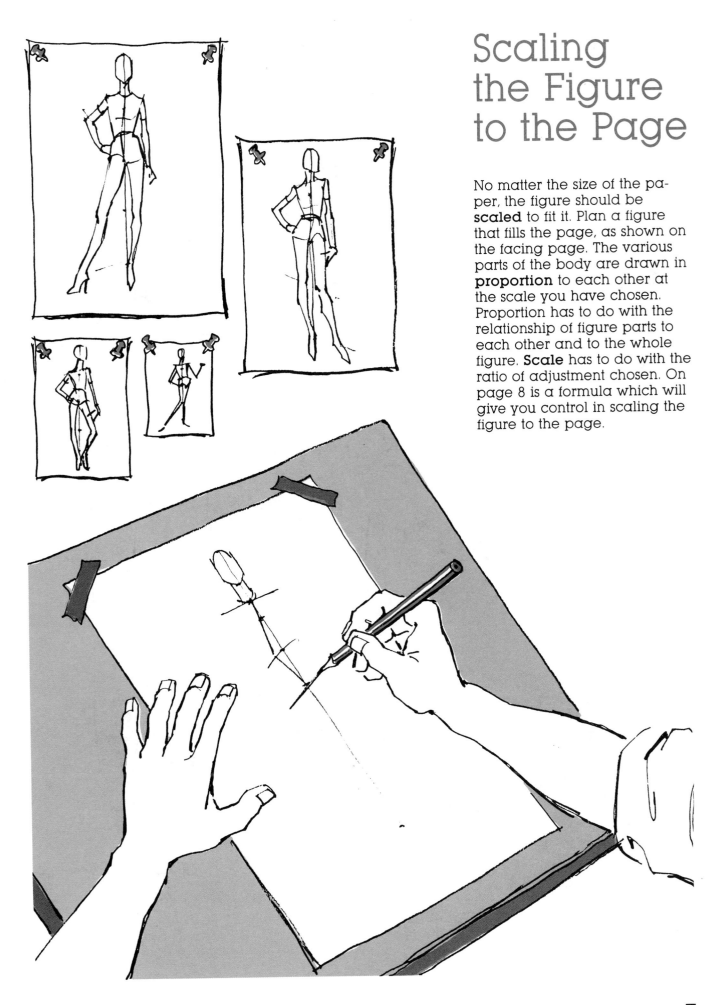

Seeing the Figure as Familiar Shapes

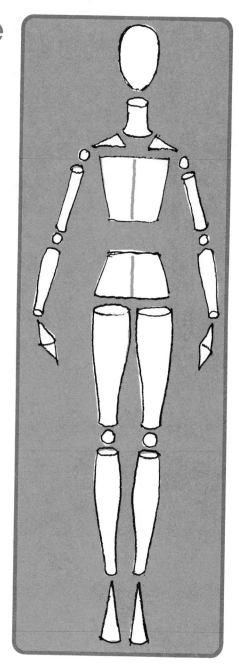

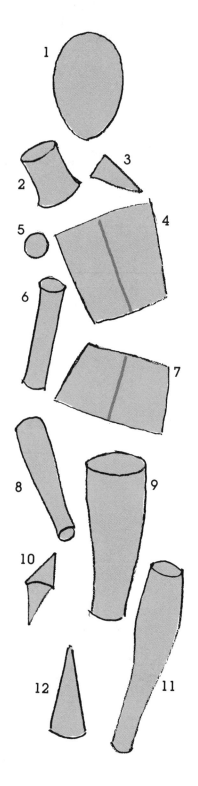

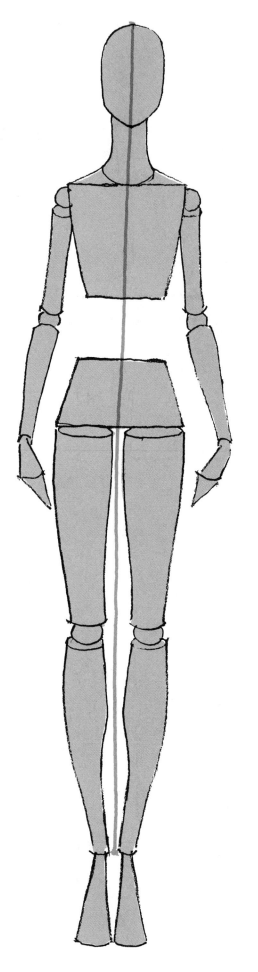

1. HEAD—egg-shaped
2. NECK—cylinder
3. SHOULDER SLOPE—wedge-shaped
4. RIB CAGE—tapered box
5. ELBOW—ball joint
6. UPPER ARM—cylinder
7. PELVIS—tapered box
8. FOREARM—tapered cylinder
9. THIGH—tapered cylinder
10. HAND—diamond-shaped
11. CALF—tapered cylinder
12. FOOT—cone-shaped

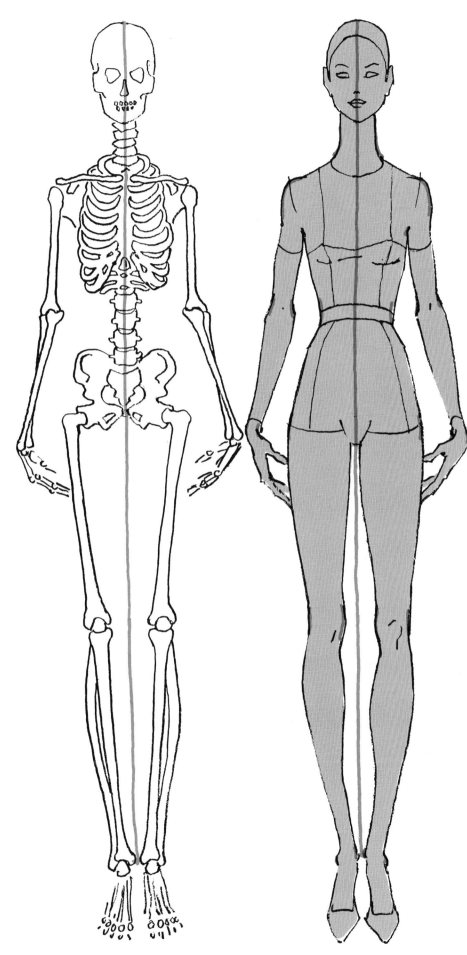

Relating the Shapes to the Skeleton and the Body

The shapes figure is shown on the facing page so that it can be compared to the two anatomical structures on this page: the skeleton and the fleshed-out figure. The shapes figure is a simplified version of the two anatomical structures. When planning the fashion figure, keep in mind the shape of each body part and the fact that the human body is three-dimensional. To draw fashion, you need a good sense of the body's form and structure.

Note the joints on the figure where the body naturally bends (marked in red). As you draw a fashion figure, use these joints as *destinations*, or points to draw to. The use of destinations will give your line a greater authority.

Planning the Figure on the Page

The formula below will let you control proportion and scale.

1 Place a mark close to the page top—A. Allowing for the bottom margin and the feet, mark B. Lightly draw a vertical line (the **plumb line**) from A to B. Divide the vertical in half and mark C.

2 Halving the line from A to C, mark 1. Divide line A-1 in half and mark 2; divide line C-1 in half and mark 3; finally, halve line B-C and mark 4.

3 Draw the head shape from A to 2. Across the middle of line 1-2, draw a horizontal line for the top of the rib cage (collarbone). Where the collarbone crosses the plumb line is the pit of the neck. At equal distances above and below 3 (waist), draw horizontal lines. Also draw a line across C. Add the sides of the rib-cage shape, tapered toward the waist, and the sides of the pelvis shape, tapered out from the hip top. Be sure all shapes match on both sides of the plumb line; then add the fist shape on the hip.

4 Now mark for each joint and draw to it. First draw the *shoulder ball joints,* then the *shoulder slopes.* (The shoulders should be two head widths wide.) Draw the *upper-arm cylinders.* Centering an imaginary compass at the pit of the neck, draw an arc from the waist to indicate *elbow* placement. Draw the *elbow joints,* then the *forearm cylinders.* Next, draw the *waistband,* connected to the rib cage and pelvis. Draw the *knee ball joints* and the *thigh cylinders.* Then draw the *calf cylinders* and add the *foot cones*—about the length of the head. Note that the wrist of the extended arm is just below C. The hand shape extends from the wrist.

Now view your work from a distance and make adjustments to please your eye.

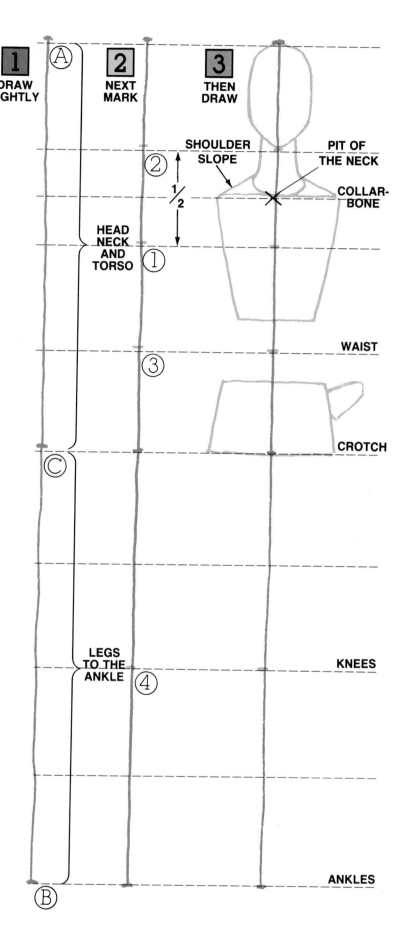

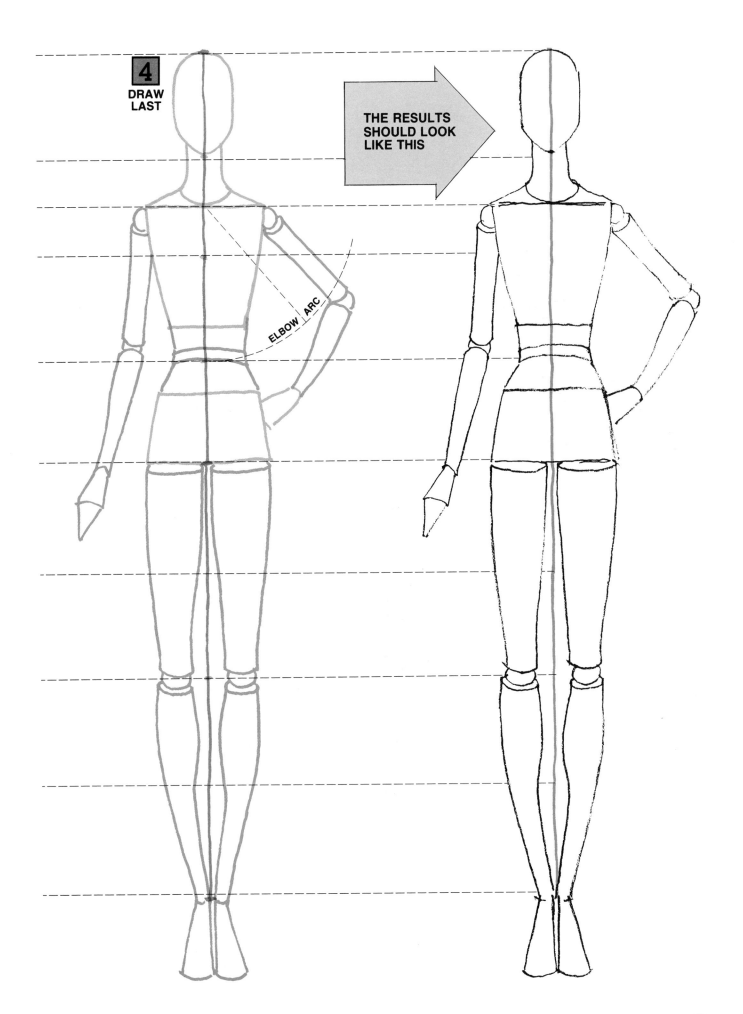

4
**DRAW
LAST**

THE RESULTS
SHOULD LOOK
LIKE THIS

ELBOW ARC

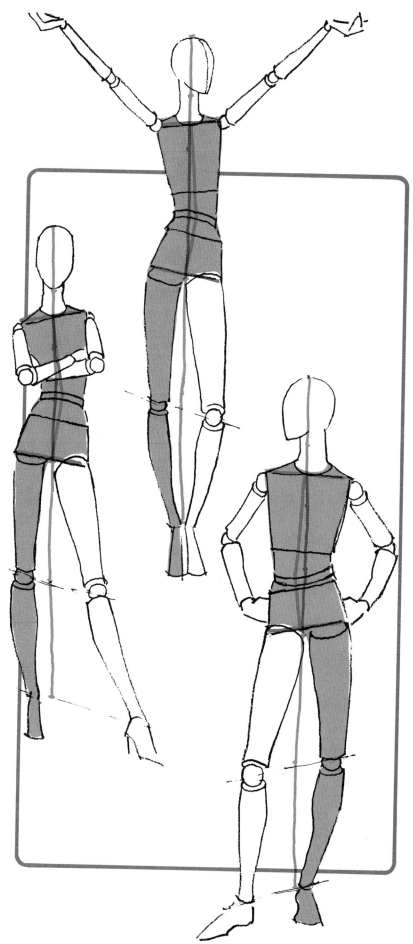

Motion Through Balance of Weight

☐ Shapes/Figures

To achieve the appearance of relaxed motion in a standing pose, draw the balance of the torso's weight resting over one foot or the other.

The weight-bearing foot should be drawn under the pit of the neck. A chain reaction then results: The hip on the weight-bearing side of the torso raises, tilting the pelvis toward the non-weight-bearing side. Reacting to the pelvic tilt, the plumb line of the torso bends at the waist as the rib cage and shoulders relax toward the weight-bearing side of the body.

The weight-bearing foot and leg, the pelvis, the waist, and the rib cage must be carefully placed to maintain the figure's balance. However, the head, neck, arms, and non-weight-bearing leg are free to create a wide variety of relaxed poses.

This formula for showing motion through balance of weight is a useful rule—but there are exceptions to it. Later you will learn to deal with rule-breaking poses. For now, concentrate on mastering this technique.

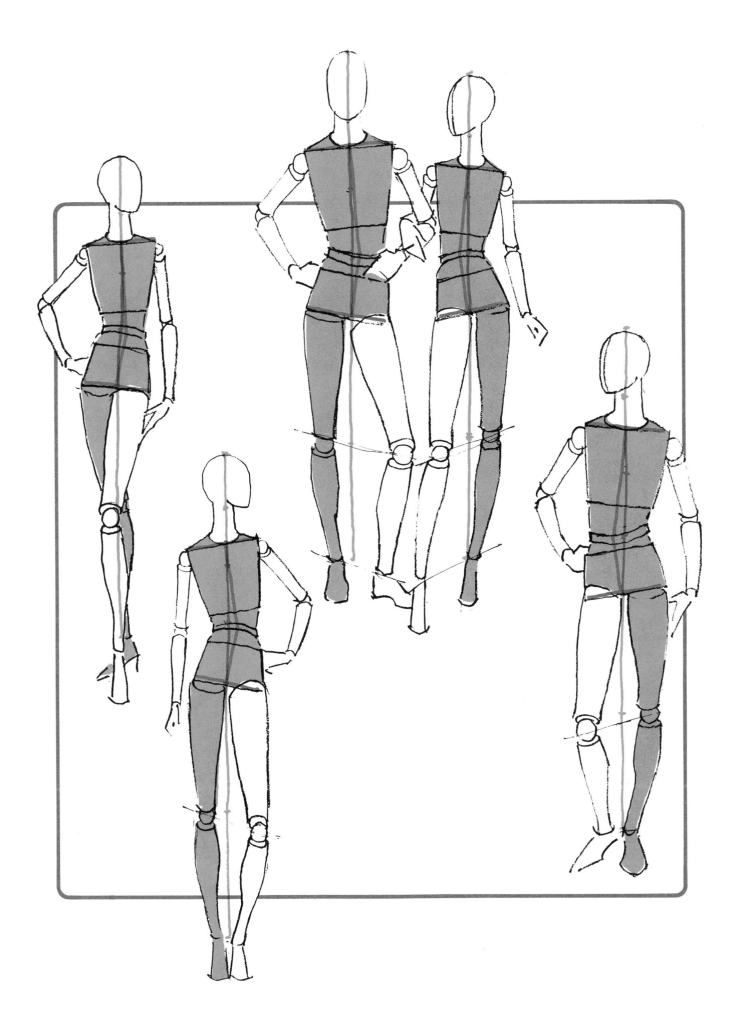

Balance of Weight

1 Draw the centerline, or plumb line, from head to ankle and mark A, B, and C and 1, 2, 3, and 4.

2 Draw the head, the neck cylinder, and the weight-bearing foot. Next, draw the rib-cage top (collarbone line) at a slight tilt, dropped toward the weight-bearing side of the figure. To establish a new, relaxed-torso centerline, or T line, draw a line at a right angle to the collarbone from the pit of the neck to the waist (3), returning to the plumb line at C. At C, draw the bottom of the pelvis shape at a right angle to the lower portion of the new, relaxed-torso centerline.

3 Above the waist, indicate the rib-cage bottom by drawing a line parallel to its top. Below the waist, indicate the pelvis top by drawing a line parallel to its bottom. Matching the shapes on each side of the centerline, complete the pelvis and rib-cage shapes. Tilt the waistband at the same angle as the pelvis. Draw the knee ball joint at 4, slightly to the right of the original plumb line. Draw the thigh cylinder from the pelvis, tapering to the knee ball joint. Now draw a calf-shaped cylinder from knee to ankle. Draw the shoulder slopes; set the fist shape on the hip.

4 Draw the shoulder ball joints. Then draw an arc crossing the waist. Using the pit of the neck as the pivotal point, position the elbow ball joints. Draw the upper-arm cylinders. Then indicate the wrist of the extended arm just below C. From the elbow ball joints, draw the forearm cylinders to both wrists. Add the hand shape. Draw a light guideline parallel to the pelvis bottom through the weight-bearing knee at 4; place the non-weight-bearing-knee ball joint. Draw another tilted guideline at ankle level to show the placement of the non-weight-bearing foot; place the foot shape and leg.

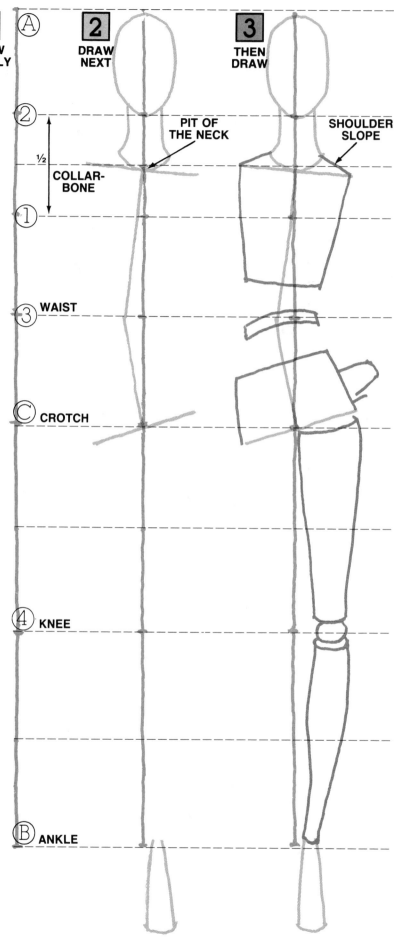

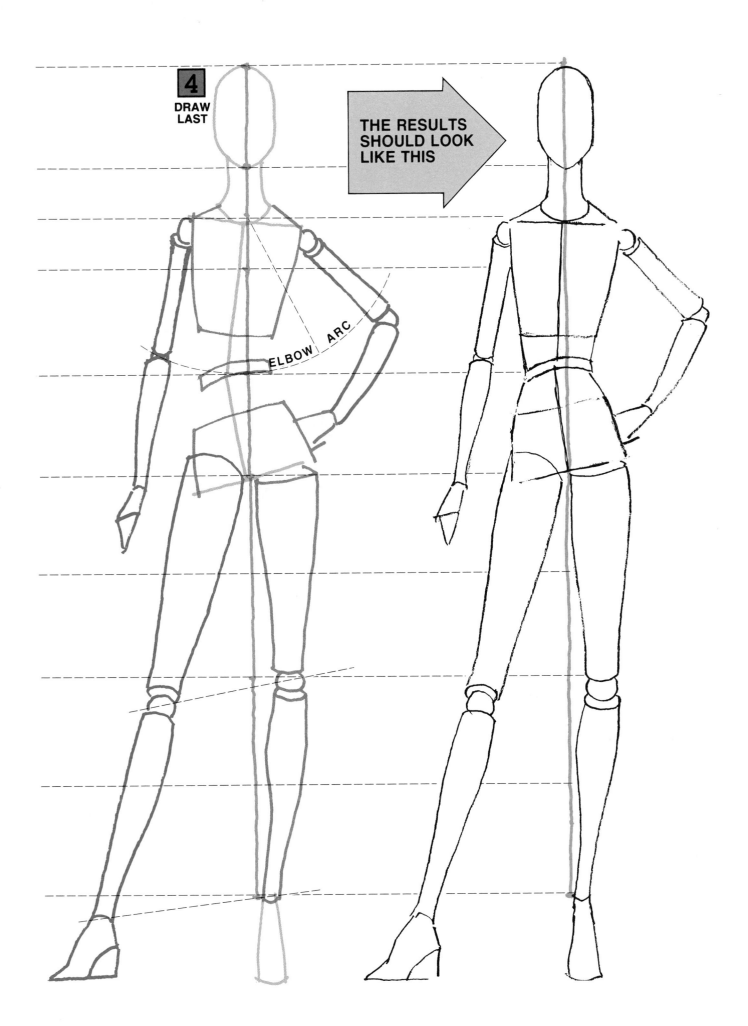

4
DRAW
LAST

THE RESULTS
SHOULD LOOK
LIKE THIS

ELBOW ARC

Turning the Figure

□ ¾ View

Turning the figure makes possible a whole new group of poses. Variations on the ¾ view are probably the most used of all poses. As the figure is turned, more key contour lines can be indicated. An extreme turn can reveal both front and back detail.

1 For the proportions of the ¾ figure, as for other figures, begin by drawing and marking the plumb line. Because turning the figure angles the neck and moves the head, draw the head shape a bit to one side of the centerline, adjusting the neck cylinder to the head placement as shown. Then draw the relaxed-torso centerline, using the sequence explained on page 12. Because the ¾-view figure is turned away from the viewer, the rib-cage and pelvis shapes are drawn narrower than those of the full-front figure.

2 Add the shaded side portions to the rib-cage and pelvis shapes. These are shaded for your information so that you can tell the front from the side. Leave an opening in the rib-cage side for attaching the arm cylinder. Draw the shoulder shapes and tilt the waistband parallel to the pelvis, as shown. Then draw the weight-bearing foot and leg.

3 As you finish the figure, remember to place the hands where you want them before drawing the arms. Also, note how the curved ends of the bent-arm cylinders are reversed from those of the full-front figure. Note, too, how the rib cage overlaps the far arm at the shoulder.

PIT OF THE NECK

SHOULDER SLOPE

ELBOW ARC

Pelvic-
Thrust
Stance

This pose is a rule breaker: The shoulders are straight yet the pelvis is tilted, resulting in a slouchy fashion stance. Variations of this look have been a mainstay of fashion modeling for years.

1 Draw and mark the vertical centerline for figure proportions. Then draw the head shape a bit to one side of the plumb line. (Again, as for the ¾ view opposite, the angled neck moves the head.) Adjust the neck cylinder to the head placement. Draw a horizontal collarbone line. Then from the waist (3) to the crotch (C), establish a new pelvis centerline to tilt the pelvis. (Note that this pose has only one tilt, as compared to the two-tilt poses you have been working on.) Now add the narrow rib-cage and pelvis shapes that show the figure is not facing directly forward on the page.

2 As you did for the ¾-view figure opposite, add the shaded side portion to the rib-cage and pelvis shapes, leaving an opening in the rib-cage side for attaching the arm cylinder. Then draw the shoulder slopes and tilt the partly shaded waistband parallel to the pelvis. Lightly indicate the weight-bearing leg and foot.

3 Once again, place the hands and feet where you want them. Then connect them with the arms and legs. Note the reverse slope of the knees where the legs overlap.

See page 26 for fleshed-out versions of these stances.

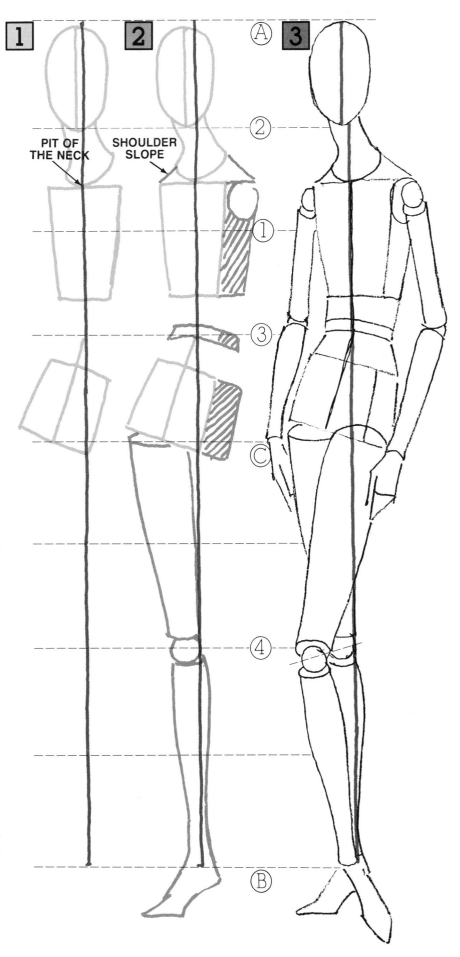

PIT OF THE NECK

SHOULDER SLOPE

Back View

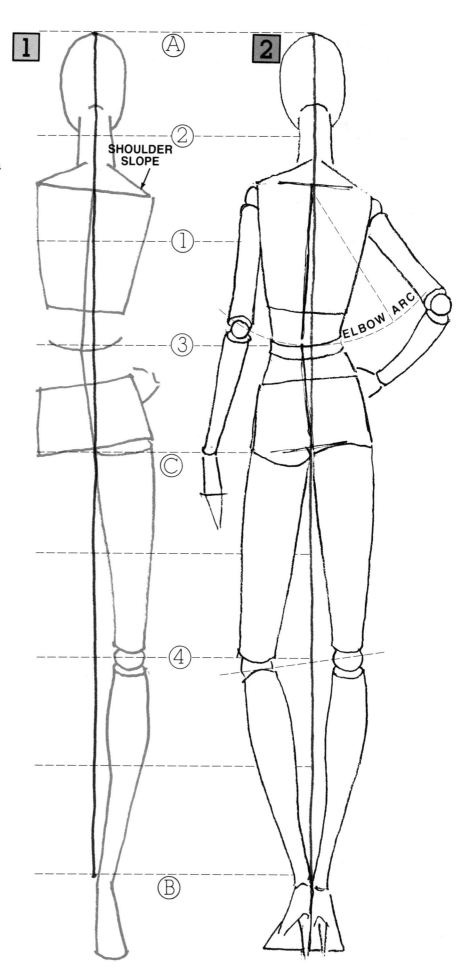

Each new pose adds to your knowledge of drawing the fashion figure. Don't be impatient to move too fast. Follow each set of sequences as given and work thoughtfully. Also, note that each pose has subtle differences from other poses and must be practiced. For instance, in the back view at right, notice how different the head shape is from the head shape of the front- and ¾-view figures. The neck cylinder rises much higher. That is because you see more neck from the back—as the chin doesn't hide it.

1 After drawing and marking the plumb line for the back-view figure, draw the head shape and neck cylinder. Then relax the centerline as you have been doing since page 12. Then work in the following sequence: rib-cage and pelvis shapes; shoulder slopes and waist tilt; weight-bearing foot and leg; hand shape set on hip.

2 As you finish your drawing, pay particular attention to the limb cylinders and the elbows. Note that they are reversed from those of the full-front pose. The elbows extend from the page toward the viewer.

See page 27 for a fleshed-out version of this pose.

SHOULDER SLOPE

ELBOW ARC

Side View ▣1

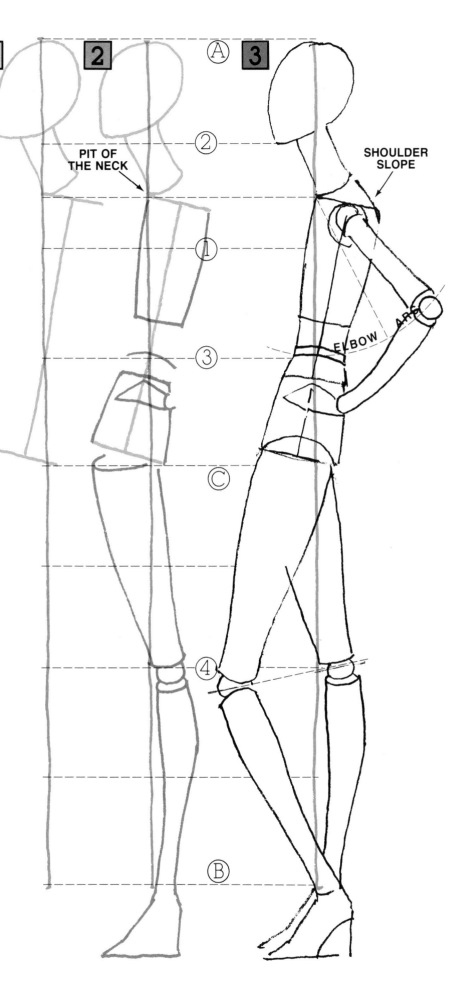

The side view—the least used pose of all—involves an entirely different perspective on the human body than do the poses you have been studying. You will no longer be able to rely on the torso centerline but will have to work from a side seam line which serves the same function. Drawing the head, neck, and torso will involve you in a fresh look at figure shapes and proportions.

1 Draw and mark the plumb line for vertical figure proportions. The profile head shape resembles a tilted egg; the neck cylinder adjusted to it is attached to the front of the body. The top of the rib cage is now depicted with a line slanting from the plumb line. Note how the side seam line starts from the top of the rib cage, crosses the plumb line at the waist (3), and ends at C. From C, add the bottom line of the pelvis shape as shown. *The torso is shaped as two Ts attached at their bases, the bottom one upside-down— one T for the rib cage and one for the pelvis.*

2 Now develop the rib-cage shape with the armhole. Then draw the pelvis shape and waist tilt. Add the weight-bearing leg and foot as well as the shape of the hand on the hip. (As you draw the pelvis, tuck the buttocks *in*.)

3 Finish drawing the figure as shown. Give special attention to the limb cylinders and elbow arc. A fleshed-out version is shown on page 27. *Now you have practiced drawing the basic shapes of the body from all the most important angles. You can see that moving the fashion figure adds drama, excitement, and personality to a sketch.*

PIT OF
THE NECK

SHOULDER
SLOPE

ELBOW

ARC

Contour

☐ Indicating Volume Through Contour Lines

To draw a successful fashion figure, think in terms of *volume*. Garments surround the figure. Contour lines serve as a reminder that your shapes are three-dimensional. These lines involve *perspective*, or representing space relationships as they appear to the eye. Contour lines will also apply to rendering fabric patterns.

Figure 1 shows the full-front figure ringed by contour lines; some are more important than others. The key contour lines are as follows:

- *Around base of neck* (for collars, necklines)
- *Around upper arm* (for short sleeves)
- *Around wrists* (for cuffs, sleeve ends, bracelets)
- *Across apex of bust*
- *Around waist* (for belts, sashes)
- *Around top of thigh* (for shorts)
- *Around calf* (for socks, hemlines, boots)

All four figures are drawn with the horizon line at the bottom line of the torso to give the illusion of viewing the model from below, as if in a fashion show. Note that at the horizon line, the direction of the contour lines reverses.

Figure 2 shows vertical contour lines. These can suggest side seams, front closure, and bust treatment. Figure 3, the back view, shows how horizontal contour lines reverse direction when a leg is bent. Figure 4 shows the effect on contour lines of a relaxed leg. Because of the leg's forward thrust, the contour lines are reversed. You will note that on all the figures illustrated, the contour lines are adjusted to the pose.

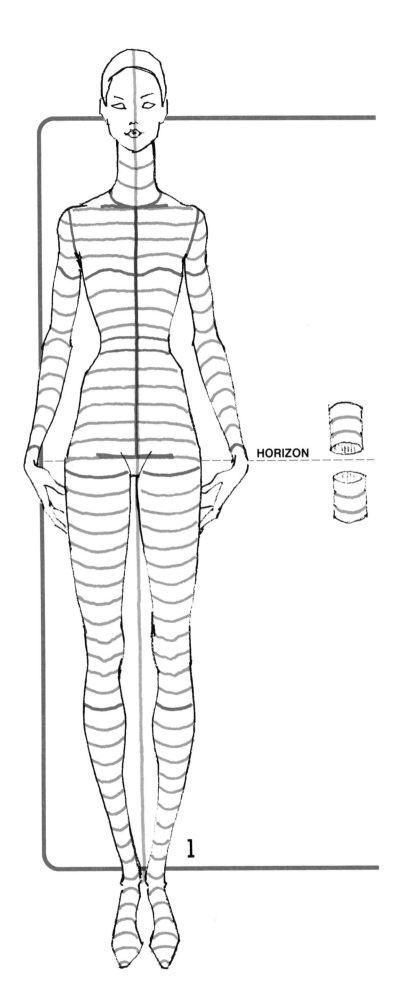

HORIZON

1

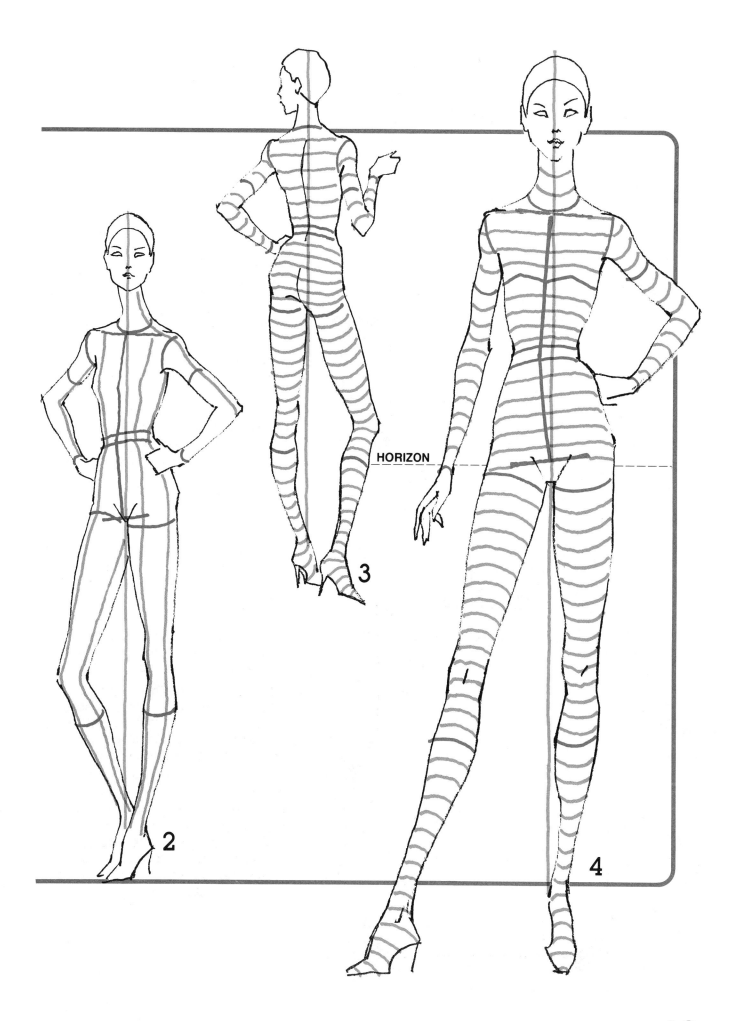

HORIZON

2

3

4

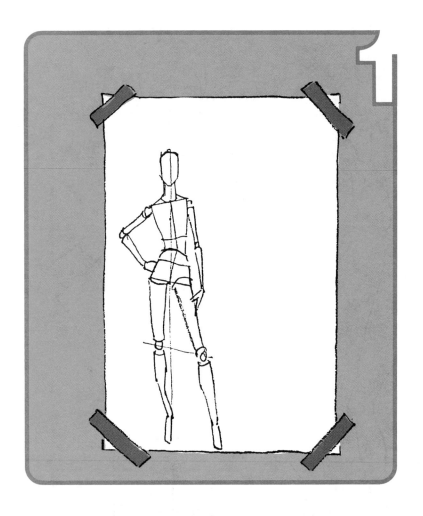

Tracing
as a
Tool

Until now, all your figures have been versions of the "shapes figure" introduced on page 6. At this point, tracing can be used as a tool to move you from the shapes figure to a fleshed-out figure. The tracing steps that follow show you a way to relieve your concern for the problems of pose, scale, and proportions so that you can concentrate on the physical characteristics of the fashion figure and the line quality of the drawing.

As you trace, try to remember you are not creating a slavish copy. Slow down. Stop and think. Let every line you make be thoughtful. You should be tracing with the following goals in mind:

1. Perfecting the placement of your figure on the page
2. Preserving the result of your work on pose, scale, and proportion
3. Giving yourself a clean **croquis,** or guide figure, to work with
4. Fleshing out your figure

The following four steps, illustrated on this and the facing page, will help ensure successful tracing.

1 Tape a drawing of a shapes figure to your drawing board. In the example shown in Figure 1, the pose, scale, and proportions have been perfected, but the placement on the page needs adjustment.

2 Tape a fresh piece of bond paper over the drawing. In Figure 2, the position of the clean paper has been adjusted to improve the placement of the figure shown in Figure 1.

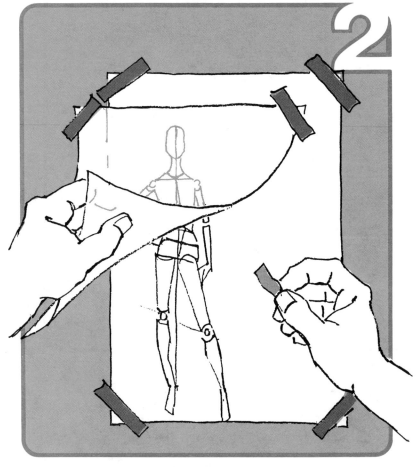

3 Using the shapes figure showing through from underneath as a guide, draw the fleshed-out figure. When translating the shapes figure into flesh, be sure to maintain a complete overview of the drawing so that all the parts of the figure will relate in shape and scale. (The following six pages will give you detailed techniques for fleshing out various shapes figures you have been drawing.)

4 Check to see whether your first tracing requires further adjustments. Trace as many times as necessary, and view from a distance until your eye is pleased with the results. The final draft should be a useful croquis over which you can draw garments. You will eventually develop a stable of croquis in various poses to show off a variety of garments.

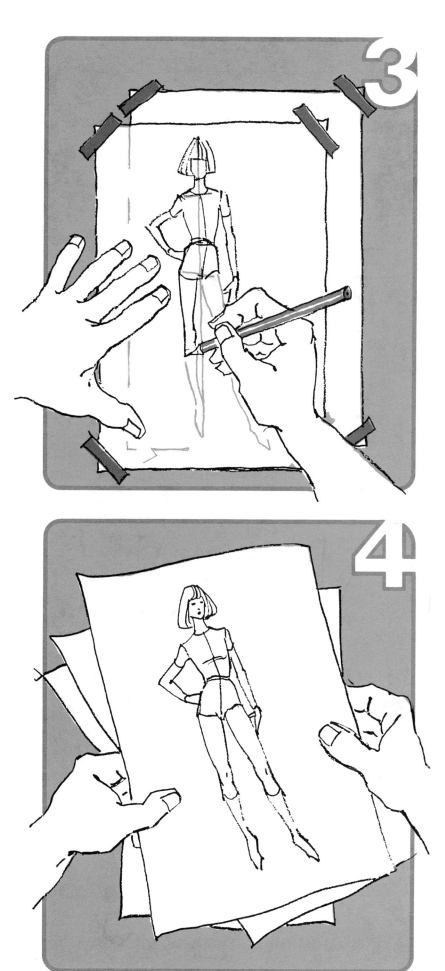

Motion Through Balance of Weight

☐ Fleshed-Out Figures

The figures on these pages were traced over the shapes figures on pages 10 and 11, using the technique explained on page 24. Note that the torsos and weight-bearing legs of Figures 1, 2, and 5 are in the same positions as those over which they were traced. The heads, arms, and relaxed legs give variation to the poses. Many other variations are possible. As you practice fleshing out the figure, try to develop many different poses. You may need to use specific stances to show certain garments at their best.

Figure 4 is an example of the inevitable exception to the rule. Although her weight is on the unbent leg, her shoulders are level. Only her hips are tilted. She is in the pelvic-thrust stance.

Another rule breaker is Figure 8. The torso is drawn as though the weight were on the right foot, but the legs have been spread for an active sportswear look. Like the other fleshed-out figures on these pages, the rule breakers were drawn over the shapes figures in the original formula poses. Then adjustments were made to alter the poses.

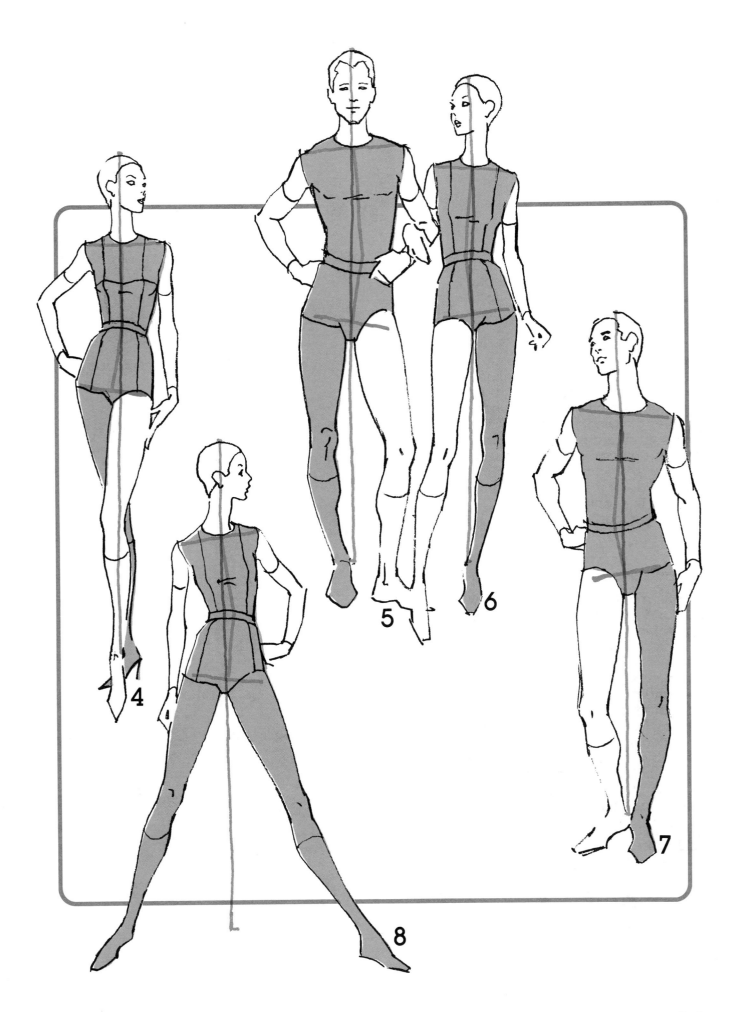

4

5

6

7

8

Fleshing Out the Figure

☐ Drawing from Point to Point

As you draw the figure, try to visualize it as a head-to-toe concept on the page. Keeping a mental image of the look to be achieved, create interim destinations (bending points) for your pencil and draw to them. Rest; then plan ahead again. When you know your destination, you can concentrate on the quality of the line which defines the shape you are drawing. Good destination points—rest-and-plan stops—are at bending places: elbows, wrists, the waist, knees, and ankles. The major advantage of the destination technique is the control of lines and shapes you can achieve with it.

1 Lightly plan a figure on the page, or trace over one of your successful shapes figures.

2 Start at the top and work down and from left to right to avoid smudging. Work from right to left if you are left-handed. Mark each destination point (listed above) in advance and draw to that point. Rest and plan ahead. Concentrate on reproducing the fleshed-out shapes. Note the arc of the waistline tilted with the pelvis. Note also the pubic triangle from the bottom line of the pelvis shape, extending the lower torso. Be sure to leave some space between the legs.

3 When you have fleshed out the figure, add the **garment construction lines** (key contour lines) as shown. They will help you place bust darts and vertical princess seam lines. The front centerline will tell you where to locate closures such as zippers and buttons. Button closures will overlap this line.

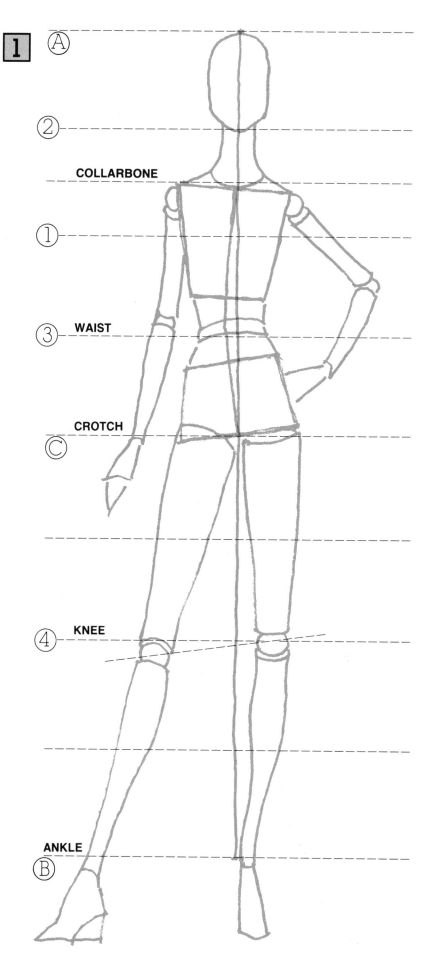

COLLARBONE

WAIST

CROTCH

KNEE

ANKLE

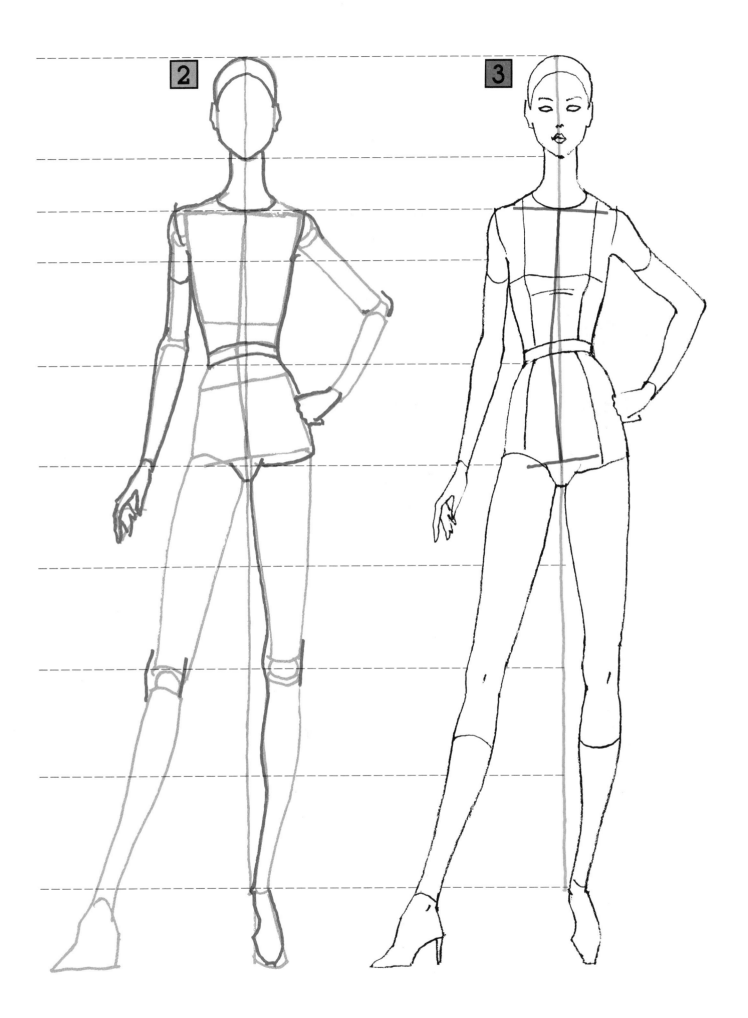

2

3

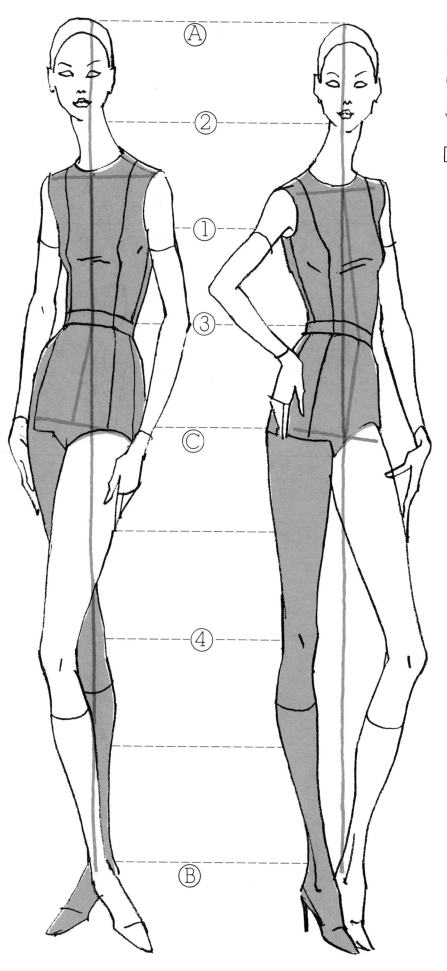

☐ Fleshed-Out

Ⓐ

②

①

③

Ⓒ

④

Ⓑ

Side View and Back View

☐ Fleshed-Out

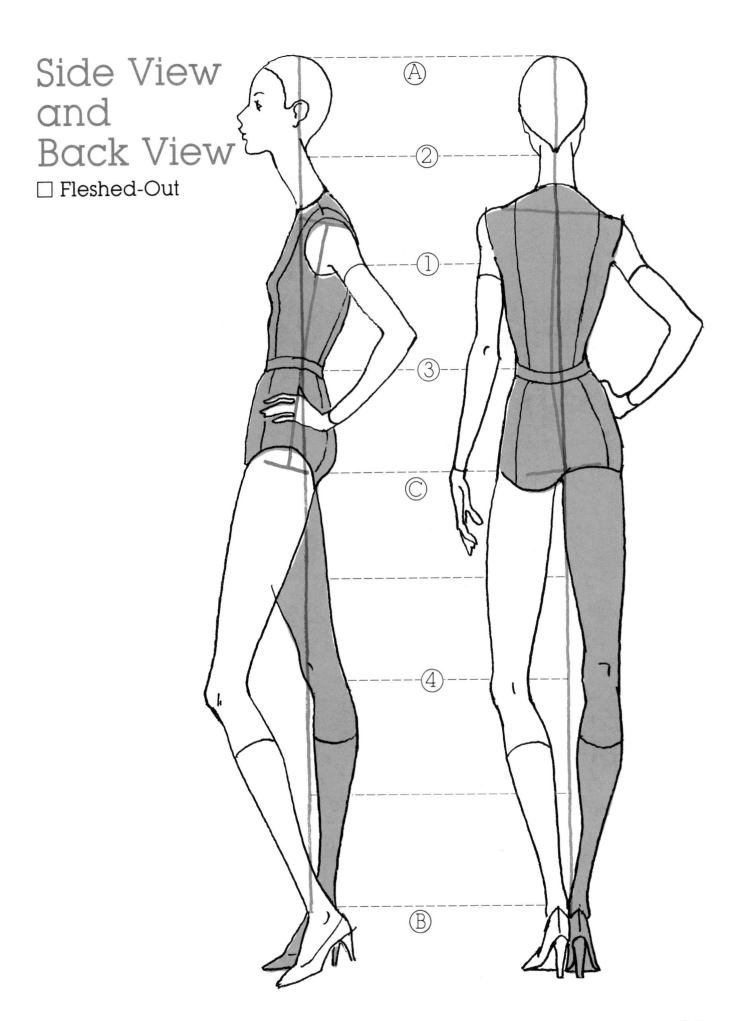

Ⓐ

②

①

③

Ⓒ

④

Ⓑ

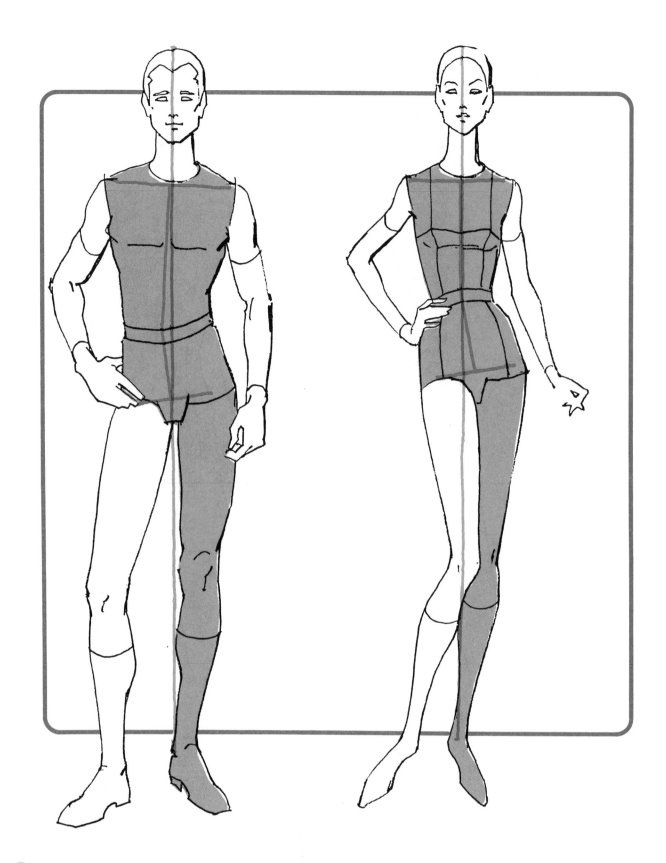

Comparing Stances

■ *Male:* square shoulders; elbows away from torso; wrists and hands less flexible; hand low on hip; fingers curve under relaxed hand; tilt of hips understated; solid stance

■ *Female:* relaxed shoulders; elbows close to torso; flexible wrists; wrist of relaxed hand bent; pronounced tilt of hips; light stance— bent knee often points inward.

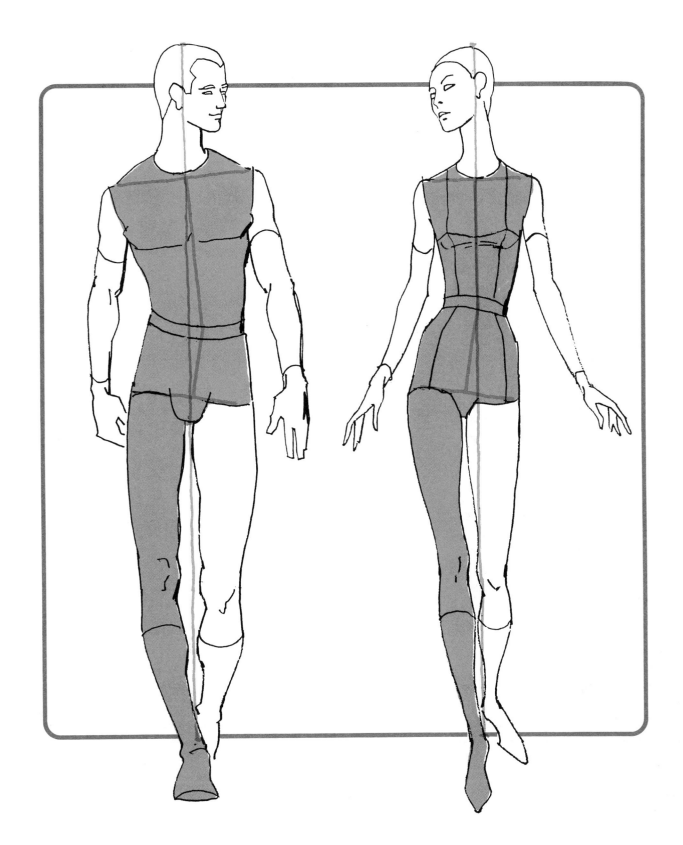

Comparing Movement

- *Male:* rolls shoulders; weight placed solidly on heels; hips move very little; arms swing freely; elbows away from torso; hands almost brushing thighs

- *Female:* moves hips more than shoulders; takes light steps, swinging bent leg out from knee; arm swing graceful; elbows held close to torso

Planning the Male Figure

The male fashion figure should be lean, athletic, and well-muscled but not bulky. The formula you have been using to plan the female fashion figure will work for the male too. The following adjustments will change the gender of the formula figure from female to male:

- Widow's peak and slightly receding hairline (less receding for under 30, more for over 30)
- Heavier brow and squarer jaw
- Thicker neck and broader shoulders
- Torso tapered to narrower hips
- Waistband curved down rather than up but still tilted with the hips
- Codpiece shape not pubic triangle
- Large-boned joints and well-defined muscles in arms and legs
- Blunter and thicker hands and feet

1 Lay out the figure using the basic shapes, proportions, and sequence used for the female figure. Make adjustments for the areas that change the gender of the figure to male.

2 Mark the destination points for fleshing out the figure. You may have to practice adjusting many figures before you are ready to flesh out the male (Step 3).

3 Lay a fresh sheet of paper over the figure you have been marking. Tracing thoughtfully, use the figure beneath as a guide to flesh out the male by connecting your destinations with fluent but well-controlled lines.

Remember your lines describe skin, muscle, and bones. Practice this pose and the ones on pages 32 to 35 until your confidence grows with your skill.

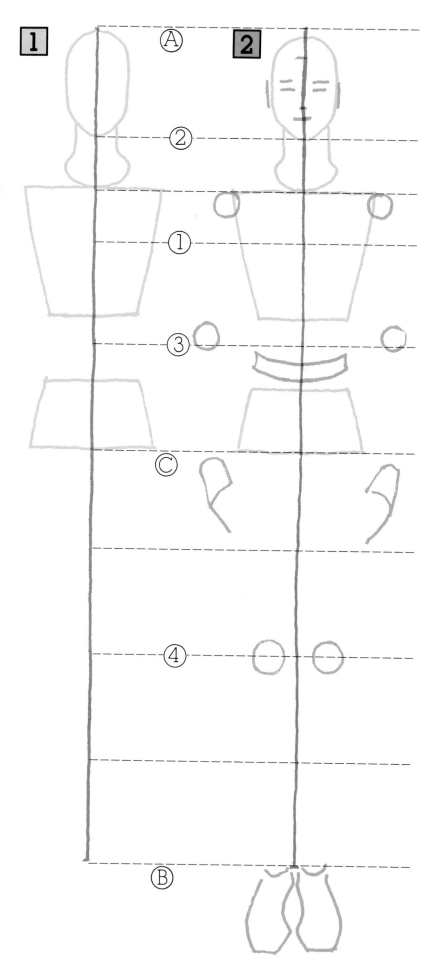

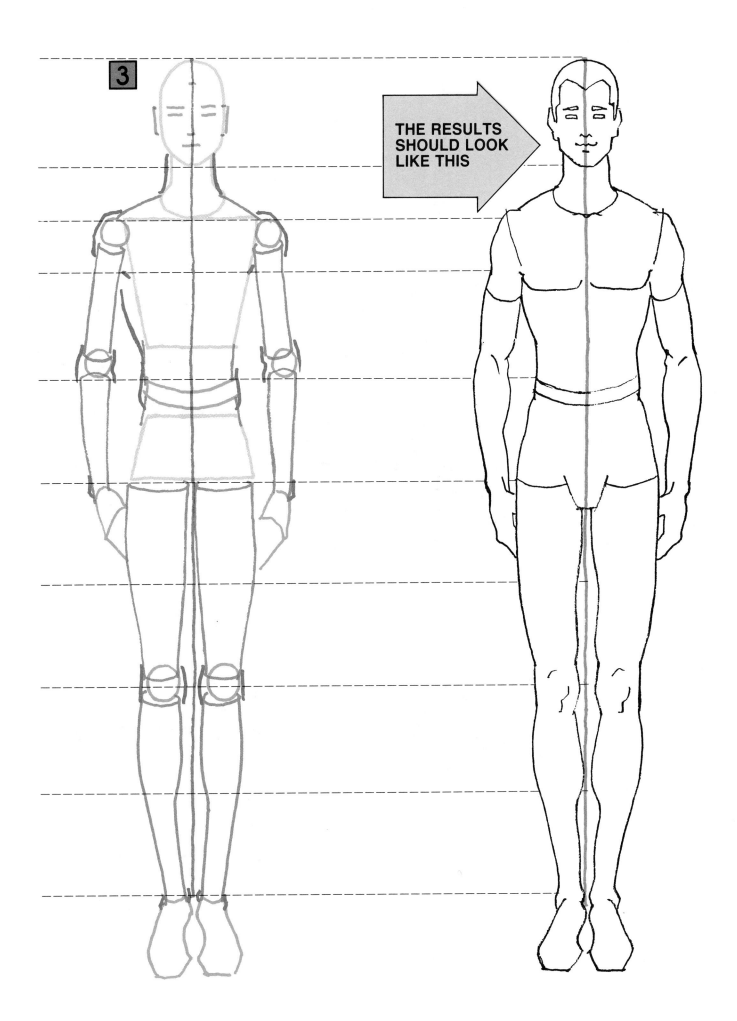

3

THE RESULTS
SHOULD LOOK
LIKE THIS

Examples of Male Stances

☐ Balance of Weight

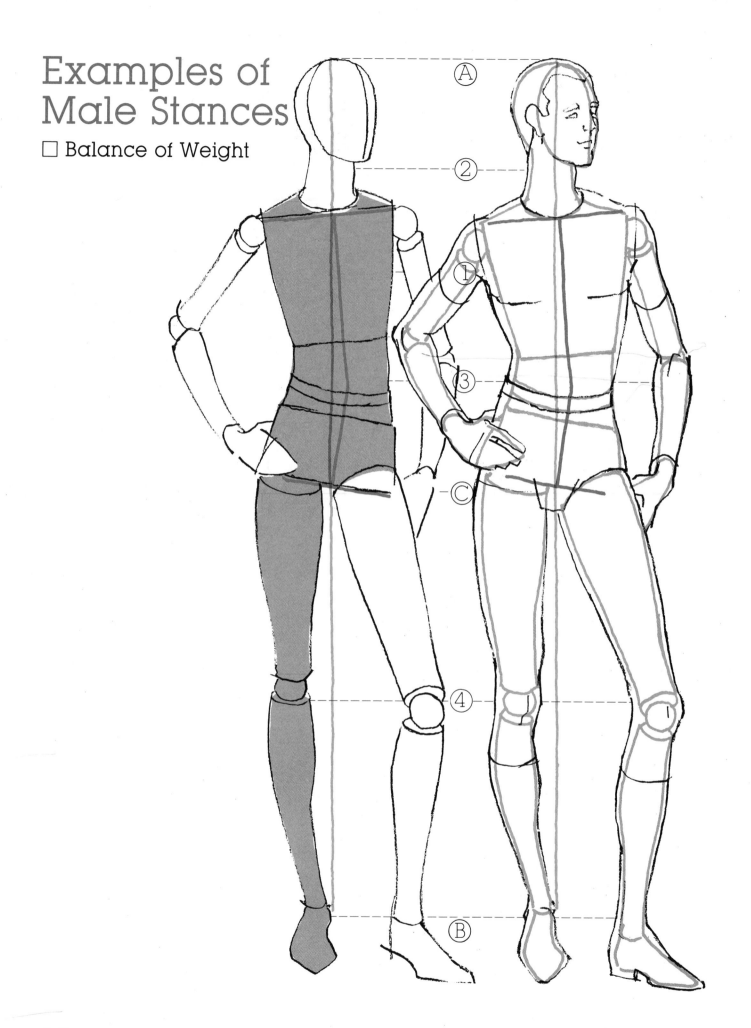

□ ¾ View

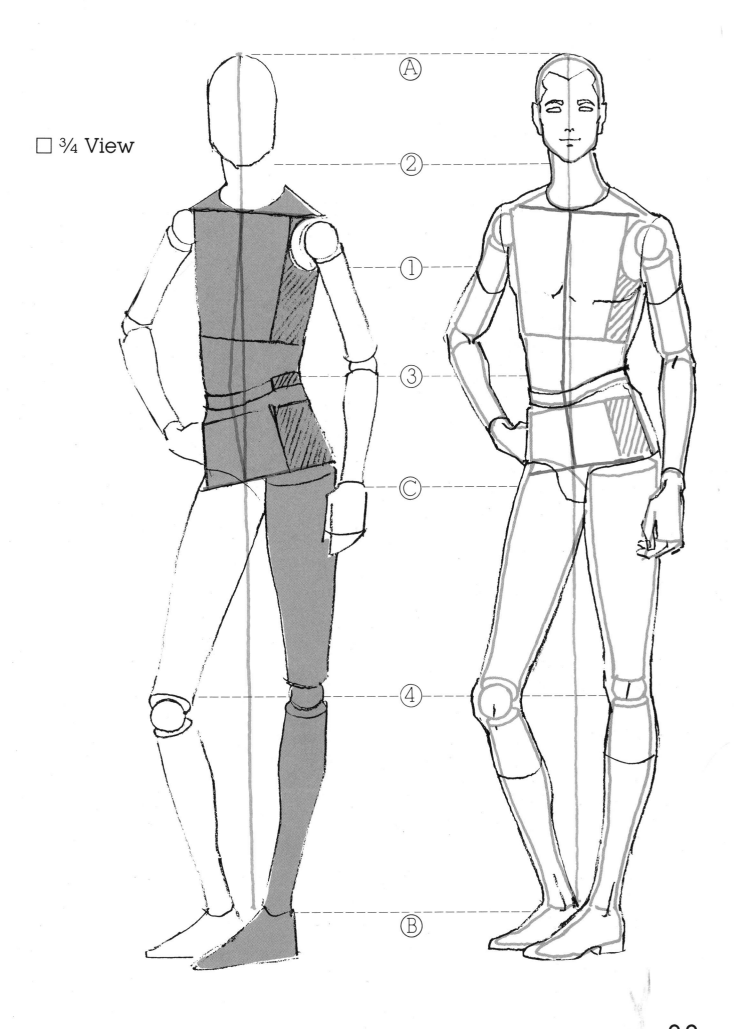

□Astride Stance

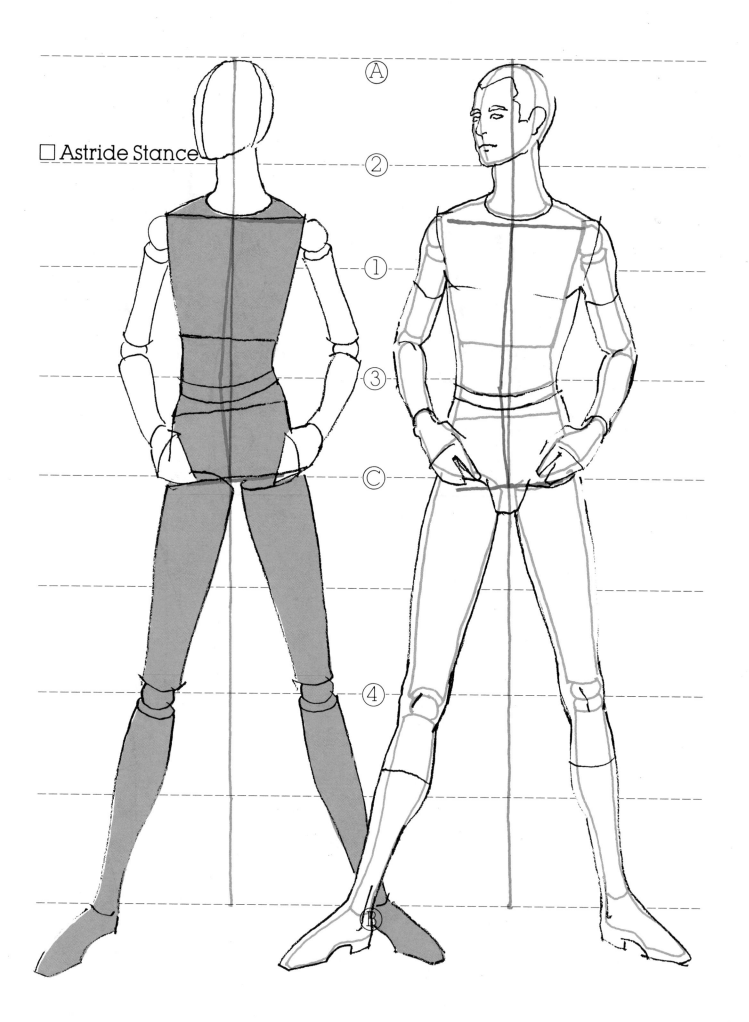

Ⓐ
②
①
③
Ⓒ
④
Ⓑ

34 Part One

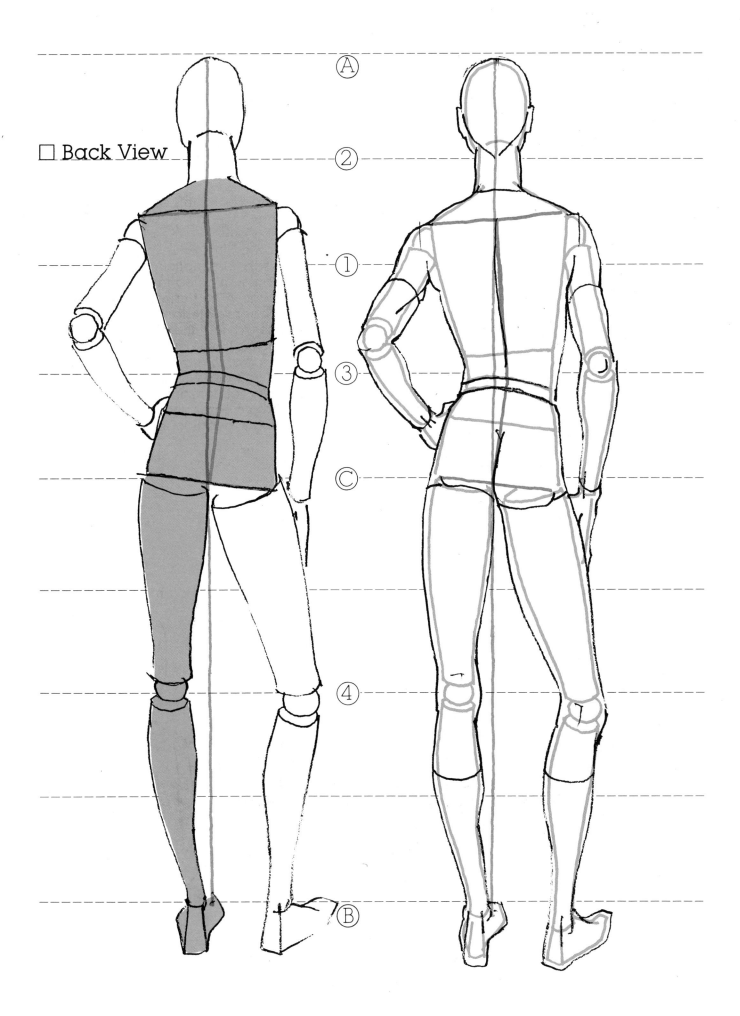

□ Back View

Ⓐ
②
①
③
©
④
ⓑ

Children's Proportions
☐ Shapes/Figures

All the figures on this and the following page have the same head size. It is understood that the head of a toddler is smaller than that of an adolescent. But for the sake of simplicity, that variable has been eliminated in the drawings on these pages. The horizontal lines on these pages relate to the head size. The fractions indicate the placement of key body points that occur between these lines. *Look at the ratio of head size to each child's body.* Study these figures *vertically,* not horizontally, and you will come to a clearer understanding of the changing proportions of children's bodies.

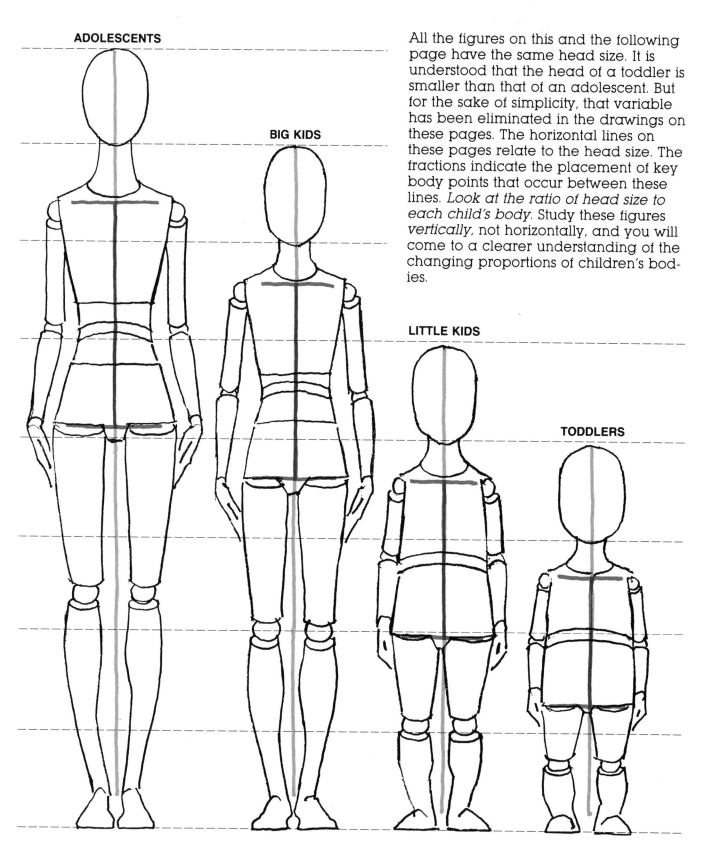

ADOLESCENTS

BIG KIDS

LITTLE KIDS

TODDLERS

Children's Proportions

☐ Fleshed-Out Figures

It is easy to see the proportional aspect of the changes children go through if we look at one ratio—head size in relation to body size. (We did not plan the adult figure as a multiple of head size because I think it is easier to scale to the *format*, or paper size and shape.) Looking at children's bodies in relation to their heads makes it easier to draw the different age groups accurately. Toddlers are typically four heads tall—plump and short legged. Little kids are five heads tall—still chubby but longer legged. Big kids, seven heads tall, are quite lean and leggy, while the proportions of adolescents—eight heads tall—forecast maturity.

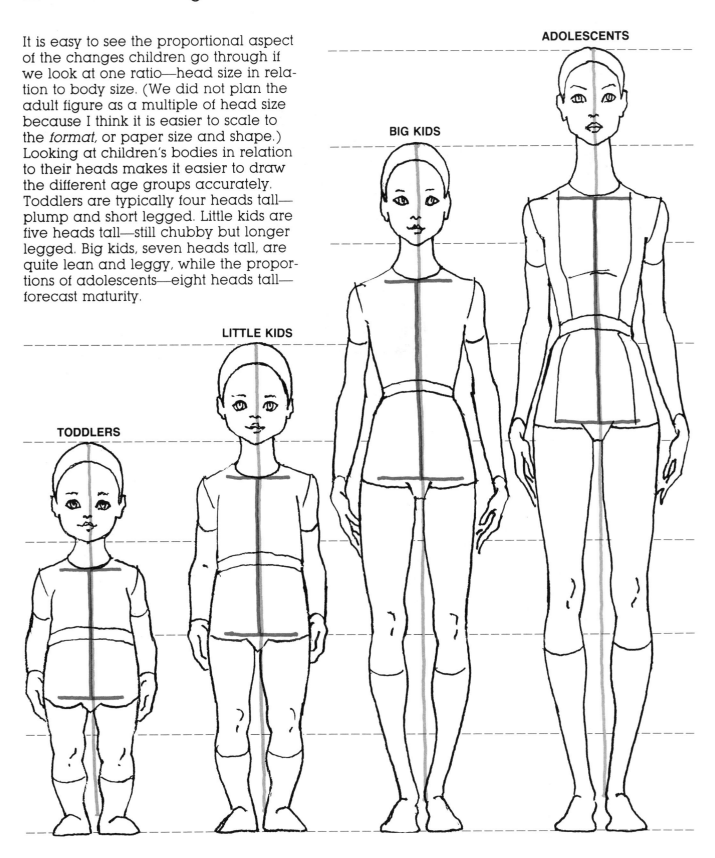

ADOLESCENTS

BIG KIDS

LITTLE KIDS

TODDLERS

Children

Toddlers

They are about 2 or 3 years old—four heads tall. Note that their facial features occupy only the lower third of their faces. Toddlers are drawn with a wide stance to show how unsteady they are on their short, chubby legs. They should look as bright, brand new, and inquisitive as kittens, reaching out and up with clumsy, chubby hands. Soft cuddly objects and pull toys do well as props.

Little Kids

They are about 4 to 6 years old—five heads tall. Their facial features still occupy only the lower third of their faces, but the features are more pronounced than those of toddlers. Little kids are growing leggier, but, like toddlers, they are drawn plump, with rounded bellies and awkward, pudgy hands. Their poses are very active—running, prancing, and marching. Their props can include balls, wagons, and scooters.

The bones of a young child are hidden in baby fat. The muscles have hardly begun to develop. Children are best portrayed by accurately conveying gesture and stance—portraying the child in motion. In addition, show the roundness of children's heads and the small shapes of their developing features.

Children

Big Kids

They are about 8 to 12 years old—seven heads tall. They have longer arms and legs. In addition, their baby fat is melting to expose the bones of knees, elbows, and other characteristics of the adult figure.

The poses typical of children in this age group often reflect exaggerated mannerisms. A coltish awkwardness affects the use of their hands and feet. Girls may behave like "little ladies" or they may be active tomboys. Boys in this age group often copy the self-consciously masculine stances and attitudes of their older idols.

For children of both sexes, sports and its associated paraphernalia can suggest poses and provide props. School also plays an important part in big kids' lives. In autumn, back-to-school props such as books, binders, and backpacks are traditional and appropriate.

Children

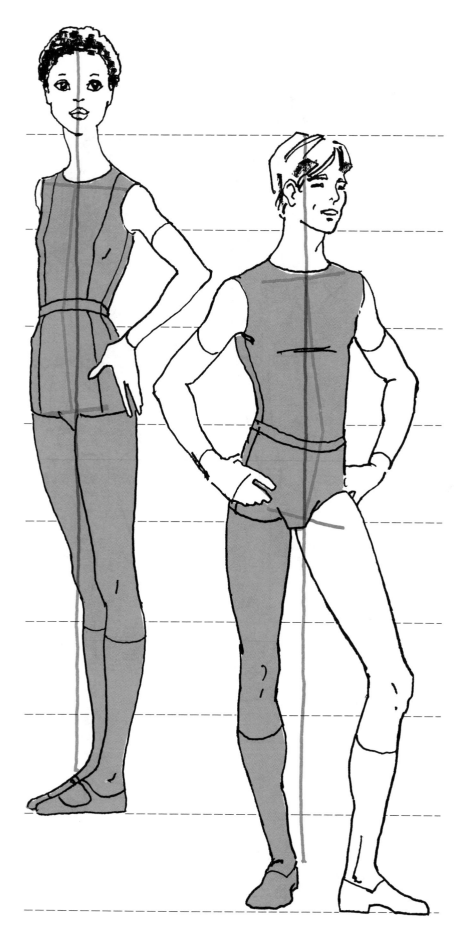

Adolescents

They are 13 to 17 years old—eight heads tall. They are leggy and slender—almost adult in their proportions. Bones may be very much in evidence.

Adolescents are interested in their appearance and grooming. Some teen clothing fads appear sloppy to adults, but to the adolescent wearing this clothing, they may be the height of peer-group chic.

Adolescents often exaggerate their own femininity or masculinity. The girls may be haughty or flirtatious. The boys often play it cool, hiding behind a macho facade. When drawing adolescents, take their affectations and attitudes into account in selecting suitable poses.

In addition to sports, school continues to occupy much time in young people's lives. Sports and school props are still appropriate. Music and dancing also loom large in importance for adolescents. Finally, the telephone is all-important for this age group.

When temps **take a dive,**

layer your look with a

cropped **cardigan,**

a polar-fleece pullover

or a **boxy car coat.**

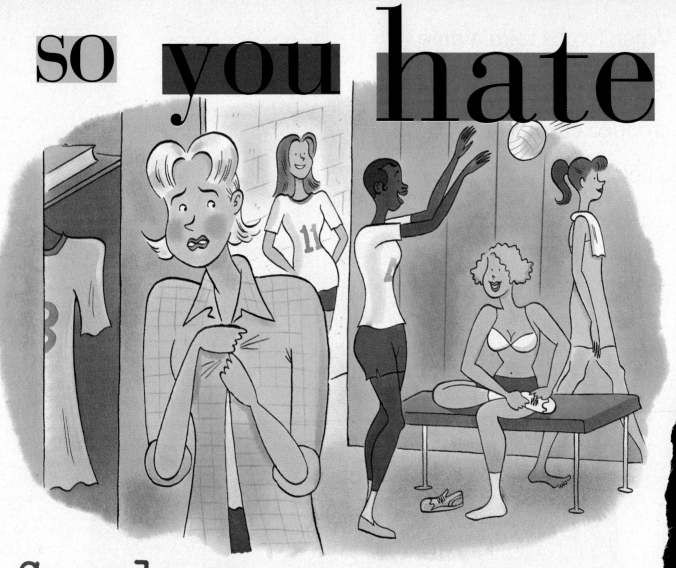

Gym class.

The words alone could give me hives. It wasn't that I hated physical activity or felt hopelessly sluggish. I just sucked when it came to gym. Last one picked for a team? That would be me. The inspiration for encouraging phrases like "easy out" and "batter can't hit"? Me again. The class, it seemed, was a minefield designed to explode what little sense of security I possessed.

In theory, moving your muscles for half an hour twice a week shouldn't be torture. (I *know* you know that occasionally pumping up your heart rate would give you a stronger body and the possibility of an endorphin high.) But somehow the prospect of playing crab-walk soccer isn't inspiring you to become a Nike poster girl. Before you start fabricating excuses so you can sit out, though, here are some survival tactics to help you get the most out of—or at least *get through*—gym class:

Nightmare #1: communal dressing

Okay, so maybe some people don't mind disrobing *en masse*, especially as they get older. But sometimes—like when you're a freshman—the mere thought of exposing lopsided breasts (or lack of any breasts at all), stomach rolls or problematic body hair is enough to cause a massive case of locker-room anxiety. Particularly if it means revealing yourself near that back-stabbing ex-friend who you know critiques every girl right down to her toenail polish.

Of course, your first instinct in such a situation is to develo[p] artful techniques to keep yourself covered. Emily, 13, fro[m] Ridgewood, New Jersey, explains: "Most of the girls hav[e] invented little ways to change without exposing themselv[es] too much, like slipping their arms out of their sleeves an[d] sliding their shirts down and off while pulling the gym shi[rt] on over their heads."

Fine, if you're a contortionist, but you're much better off [if] you can just get over it, which becomes much easier once yo[u] realize you're not the only one who's worried about bein[g] scrutinized. Shondra, 17, from Springville, Utah, says, "All m[y] life I've been overweight. I like sports a lot, but I was so para[-] noid about my weight that I hated gym—specifically, changin[g] into my gym clothes. But I've since discovered that everyone i[s] so convinced other people are looking at them that they're to[o] busy to watch anyone else." It's kind of like dancing that way[.]

So relax. Once you get over your oh-my-God-I'm-in-my[-] Barbie-panties anxiety, you may even come to appreciate the unique opportunities of the locker room. "It's where a lot of catch-up time is," says Bethann, 15, from Alameda, California. What other class allows you to hang out and gossip with other girls for the first five minutes?

Heads and Faces

☐ Female

The fashion figure's face can complete the total fashion message. It can suggest that a given clothing design is aimed at a particular age, type, or image of target customer. The fashion figure's face can also show pleasure wearing this specific design.

Presented here are typical fashion-face proportions. Study the diagram at the right; then practice drawing faces in the sequences of steps presented below.

A few words on eyes: *eyes too large*—cartoony; *eyes too close*—a mean look; *eyes too far apart*—a blank look; *white of eyes above or around iris*—fright; *too much white below iris*—sleepy.

1 Draw head shape and guidelines, and place eyes. Leave eye-space between eyes of front view. (In the ¾ view, note the diminished size of far eye, slight roundness of near eye.) Place side-view eye well forward.

2 Draw hairline; place brows, nose, mouth, using ratios above. Use judgment to place the mouth attractively. The first line you draw is the opening of the mouth, and it should be the strongest.

3 Complete the facial features. Add nose profile to side and ¾ views. Add eyelids, irises, ears, upper and lower lips, neck cylinder. Note the side-view nose and lips drawn outside head shape; upper lips overhang lower. Also note the angle of neck cylinder, placement of ear.

4 Add finishing details such as hair and eye pupils. Add makeup accents to eyes and lips.

TOP OF THE HEAD
HAIRLINE
⅓
BROW
EYES ½
EAR AND NOSE
⅓
⅓
CHIN

1 2 3 4

44 Part One

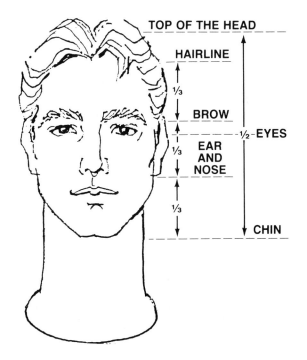

TOP OF THE HEAD

HAIRLINE

1/3

BROW

1/2 EYES

1/3

EAR
AND
NOSE

1/3

CHIN

Heads and Faces
☐ Male

The male face can be drawn using the same proportions as used for the female face. The difference between the sexes is marked by the male's narrowed eyes and his hairline receding from a widow's peak. The male face has a much heavier brow, squarer jaw, and more definite chin than the female face. More attention is paid to the male nose and less to the mouth. Also, the male's head sits on a much thicker neck cylinder.

Men and women use their eyes differently. Women enlarge their eyes with makeup, while men slit theirs to look focused, frowning more. Whether you are drawing a male or a female, remember: An overdrawn nose will dominate the face; every line adds 10 years. Be sure your practice drawings are a useful size for complete figures.

1 Same sequence as for female. Note the different guidelines for each view.

2 Same sequence as for female.

3 Same sequence as for female, but square the male's jaw and chin. Make brow heavier. In ¾ view, far half of lips is smaller than near half. Do not outline male's lips. Now refine cheekbones and chin.

4 Men's faces are allowed to have character lines to achieve a rugged, mature look.

1   2   3   4

Faces in Fashion

Until recently, the image of the fashion mannequin was exclusively caucasian. It had chiseled patrician features, a straight nose, and pale eyes. In recent years, this narrow attitude has happily changed. Contemporary fashion houses, magazines, brochures, and display windows are using models of every ethnic type to show, flatter, and create a demand for garments.

Drawing Hair

Whatever ethnic type you are drawing, you will want to take care with the hair, an important part of the total fashion message. Remember, whether hair is long, short, straight, wavy, or curly, its source is the scalp.

1 Lightly block in the silhouette of the hair, drawing the shape of the look or style desired.

2 Indicate irregularly the linear or other textural quality of the hair. Most often you will follow some individual lines of hair from the scalp to the end, as shown. Indicate whatever wavy or curly lines the hairstyle calls for. Use restraint so as not to end up with the cluttered, scribbled look of an amateur.

3 For more detail you can create **highlights** (bright spots reflecting light) with color and **dropouts** (places where color has not been applied). To produce dropouts, darken only the areas not exposed to an imaginary light source, leaving open the areas exposed to the imaginary light. This technique will give the illusion of lustrous, healthy hair.

Hand Shapes
☐ Female

The female fashion hand is a slender, elegant, and gracefully exaggerated version of the normal hand. Do not scale the hand too small. The open hand almost covers the face, with the index finger close to the length of the palm.

The process for drawing female fashion-hand shapes follows. Think of the hand as a shallow rectangular box with the thumb protruding from the side and the fingers from the end. Then turn the box.

1 Lightly draw the basic shape of the pose you have chosen.

2 Add the most prominent exposed digits (thumb and fingers).

3 Refine, and add less prominent digits.

4 Complete, but do not overdraw! Scale and the basic shapes work better than intricate anatomical detail.

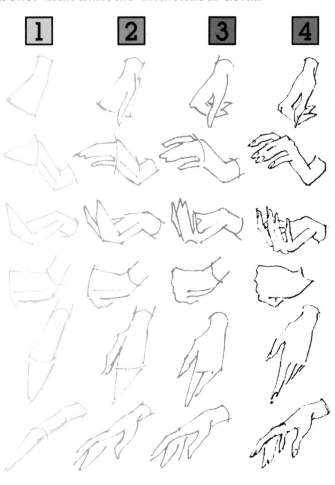

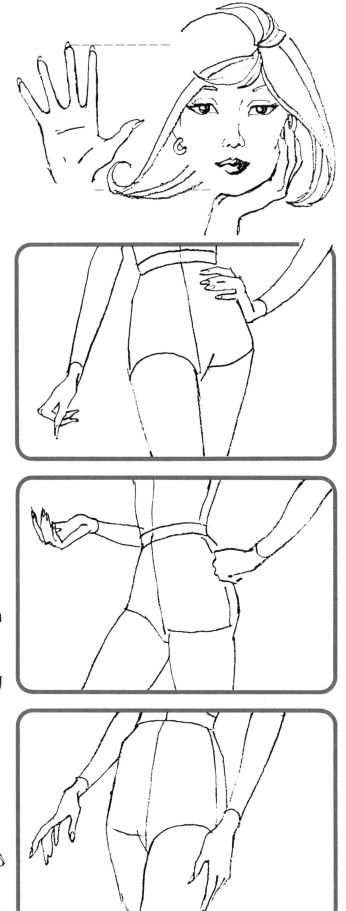

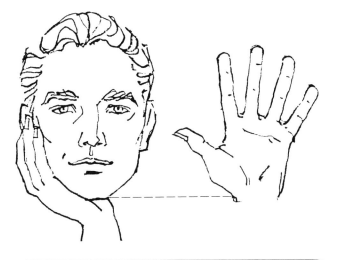

Hand Shapes

The male hand is squarer than the female hand and has blunter fingers. As in the female hand, the index finger and palm are close to the same length. When posed on the hip, the male hand rests on its fingers and thumb. When relaxed, the fingers curl inward. As in drawing the female hand, think of a shallow rectangular box with thumb and fingers.

1 Lightly draw the basic shape of the pose you have chosen.

2 Add prominent exposed digits (thumb and fingers).

3 Add less prominent fingers, and if visible, the male's knuckles and large joints.

4 Complete without overdrawing. Think scale and basic shapes.

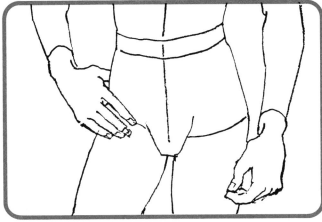

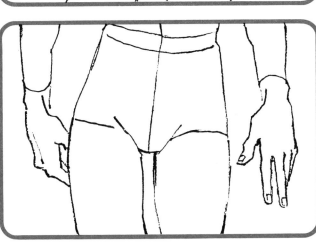

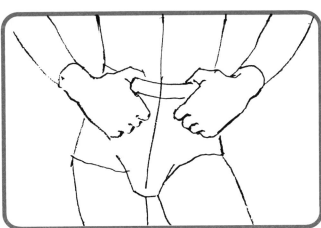

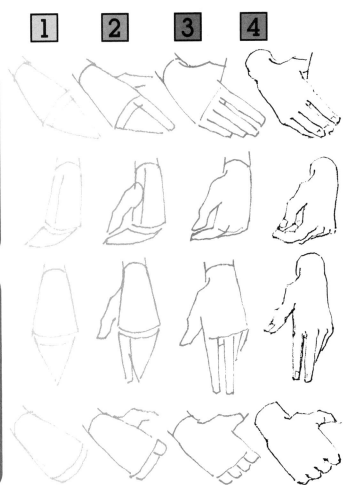

Feet/Shoes
☐ Female

Like hands, feet are scaled close to the length of the head. The higher the heel, the longer the front and ¾ views will be. For flat shoes, the front view will shorten and widen or the stance can spread. All front and ¾ views will require **foreshortening** (contraction in the direction of depth to suggest projection in space). The female fashion foot should be elegant, with delicate bones. Below are process drawings for most of the examples at the right.

1 Lightly draw the basic shape. Note the delicate ankles.

2 Indicate arch if in view, then toe shape.

3 Add details of foot and/or shoe construction such as toes, straps, and heels. Do not overdraw. Think scale and shape!

1　　**2**　　**3**

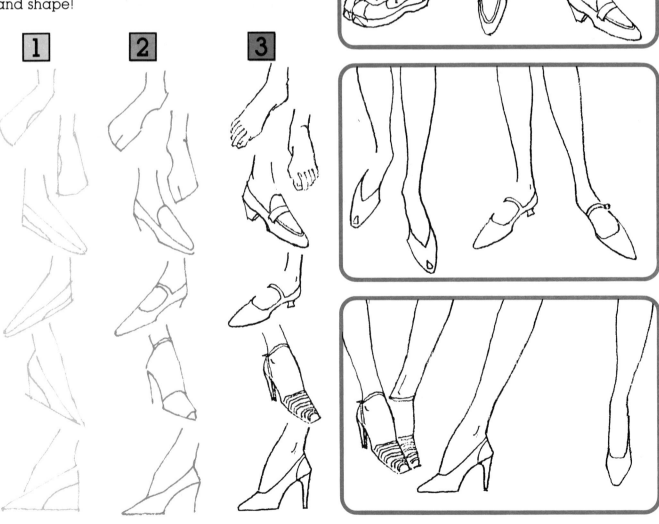

Feet/Shoes
☐ Male

The approach to drawing the male foot is much like drawing the female's, though the male foot is larger boned and has a solid stance. As with the female foot, front and ¾ views require foreshortening. At the left are samples of men's feet and shoes, and below are process drawings for them.

1 Lightly draw the basic shape. Note the heavy ankle and large bone structure.

2 Indicate arch if in view, then toe shape. For a shoe, draw the sole. Draw top and tongue if they show.

3 Add selected details such as stitching and shoelaces, but do not overdraw. Scaling and simple shapes are more important than intricate detail.

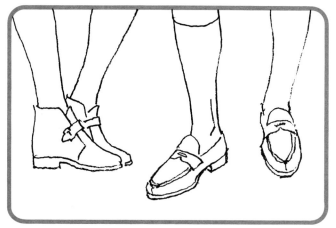

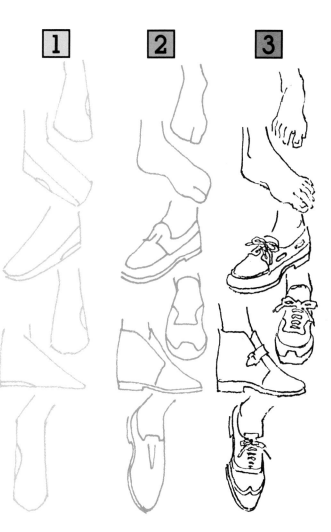

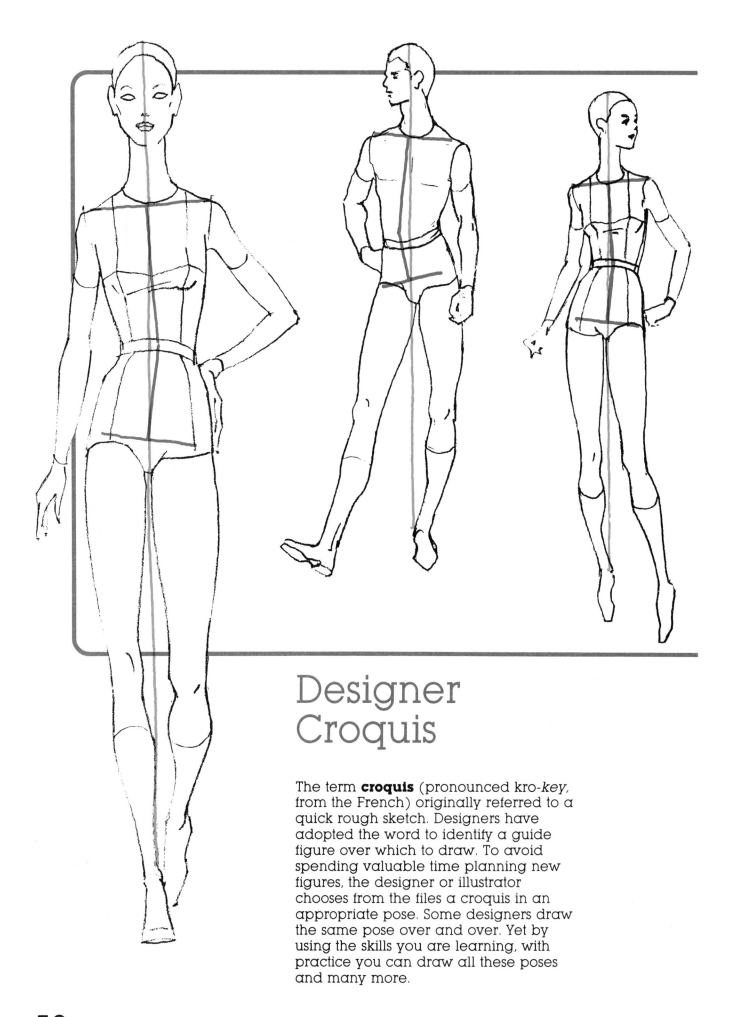

Designer
Croquis

The term **croquis** (pronounced kro-*key*, from the French) originally referred to a quick rough sketch. Designers have adopted the word to identify a guide figure over which to draw. To avoid spending valuable time planning new figures, the designer or illustrator chooses from the files a croquis in an appropriate pose. Some designers draw the same pose over and over. Yet by using the skills you are learning, with practice you can draw all these poses and many more.

Part Two
Drawing the Garments

Having practiced the figure and created a group of croquis in various poses, we can move on. Visually describing the garment with pencil or pen provides a new challenge. You will need the same discipline of practice and perseverance you needed to draw figures, but drawing garments is more fun.

Part Two opens with a discussion of the importance of silhouette. We'll see how it not only depicts its era but also forecasts fashion to come. Then we'll move on to discuss accents, which can add punch and authority to your work. We'll have more to say about tracing (rather than erasing). We'll talk about around-the-house aids you can use to help yourself. We'll promote the value of a fashion-art collection. (You'll improve your knowledge of fashion drawing and foster a personal style more swiftly if you try your hand at "copycat" drawings from your favorite fashion illustrators.) I'll also include some techniques for translating fashion photos and live models into fashion drawings.

As in Part One, the exercises are on double-page spreads for easy viewing. Again sequence and process are emphasized. (You should use a croquis for the techniques presented in the process drawings.) I show a selection of basic garments in both examples and step-by-step explanations. Practice these examples until you are pleased with the results before trying more complex designs.

Part Two also includes a gallery of women's, men's, and children's fashions that have achieved "classic" status. These styles are reintroduced with fresh interpretations every few seasons.

1902

1907

1912

Twentieth-Century Silhouettes

Shapes of clothing change often and dramatically over the years. The informed individual is able to recognize a specific era from only the **silhouette,** the fashion shape.

Examine the silhouettes shown here. Note how waistlines are cinched, eased, raised, and lowered; then the cycle repeats. Shoulders balloon, narrow, and slope, then are puffed and padded again. Skirts range from very full to pencil slim, with hemlines that move capriciously up and down.

1917 **1922** **1927** **1932** **1937**

Since the silhouette usually changes in mid-decade, the fashion at the close of one decade usually forecasts those to come in the opening years of the next decade.

1902: Women joining the office work force require business apparel such as *suits* (matching skirts and jackets). Still popular is **mono-bust line** of 1890s, a pushed-up look merging the breasts into a single shape.

1907: Corsets are eased; skirts begin to narrow; mono-bust continues.

1912: Corsets and bust lines are loosened, but **hobble skirts** (tight, long, and difficult to walk in) now constrict movement.

1917: Busy women of World War I require shorter, fuller skirts.

1922: Skirts still getting shorter; emphasis moves from bust and waist to hip.

1927: Short hair and hemlines at knee combine with low waist to create boyish flapper look.

1932: Bias cut; hemlines drop. Waistlines stay low.

1937: Natural waist returns; hemlines rise. Shoulders now padded or puffed.

1942: World War II—square-shouldered military look; short skirts conserve fabric.

1947: Dior's **New Look**—sloped shoulders; tiny waist; padded hips; full, long skirts.

1952: Waist-cinching jackets; long, slim stiletto skirts.

1957: Eased jackets, higher waistlines. Skirts still slim, but hemlines rise.

1962: the **trapeze influence**—fitted in front and eased in back to fall full from shoulders. Hemlines reach kneecap.

1967 1972 1977 1982

1967: The **miniskirt** (midthigh length) is established. A high waist, huge coiffure, and large hat and boots complete the look.

1972: As pants begin to be accepted for office wear, designers pay new attention. Not all **pantsuits** (suits with pants) are as mannish as the one shown here.

1977: The **Annie Hall Look** (eclectic, after actress Diane Keaton's clothes in a popular Woody Allen film)—otherwise unstructured jackets have padded, puffed shoulders for a boxy effect. Longer, full skirts worn with boots.

1982: Among other looks, short, fitted blazers with natural waist and puffed, or padded, shoulders appear over longer, full skirts as women become less self-conscious about expressing femininity. Eclecticism yields to pulled-together look.

By now the great value of a knowledge of fashion history should be self-evident. The earlier centuries of fashion history, as well as the twentieth century, will repay your scrutiny. You can learn more about fashion history from books and from the fashion collections of museums and libraries.

**RICHARD HOLIMANN
FOR NEIMAN-MARCUS**

Gallery of Fashion Art

with Croquis

Behind examples of *published* fashion art—the work of several artists—are the croquis from which they could have been drawn. Note how the shapes you have been practicing relate to the exaggerated stances used in these very sophisticated high-fashion drawings.

**RUTH LAUMOND
FOR GRODINS**

**MARILEE MEYER
FOR I. MAGNIN**

Drawing Flat

Among the drawings a designer must supply are flat working drawings so the staff in the workroom can coordinate the line. These flat drawings are usually swatched with fabric samples and peppered with notes on special details.

Another important use for flat drawings has arisen with the increasing use of overseas production for fashion lines. This requires sending specification drawings with the actual dimensions—length and width—of garment parts like sleeves, collars, and cuffs precisely noted. Accurately proportioned flat drawings of both front and back views, with clearly indicated details, are essential in today's international fashion world. Communication breaks down without them. Accurate measurements ensure correct manufacture far from the workroom.

To practice flat drawing, select garments from your own wardrobe, and lay them flat on the floor or any convenient horizontal surface. Copy them accurately, showing all visible construction lines and being especially careful about proportion.

The technique of drawing a garment flat is one you can master with observation and practice. You will need to practice it as much as the techniques involved in putting clothing on a figure—the focus of Part Two.

Tracing
as a
Tool
☐ Revisited

You have been using tracing to work up figures useful as croquis. When drawing garments, you can use the same tracing technique:

1. Choose a croquis in the pose you want. Place your page over it, and rough in the garment's silhouette and shapes.
2. Use your rough as a guide to draw the garment in greater detail.
3. Trace as many drafts as you need to get a clean final drawing.

If each tracing doesn't improve on the previous one, something is wrong. Back to the drawing board. Don't trace and retrace in the blind hope of improvement. Instead, try to "see" the lines in your mind's eye and project them on the page before you draw them. This is especially important for designers who are working from concepts, unlike illustrators who are working from a finished garment.

The line quality of your final draft should suggest an original drawing. It should never have a "traced" look. Tracing is not a crutch to make drawing easy, but a tool to make it cleaner and more authoritative.

Other Tools Around the House

You can practice fashion-drawing techniques at home with the tools and materials recommended on page 2. Some helpful practice aids you need to develop your skills may already be on hand. Others can be obtained at minimum expense with clever shopping.

Practice drawing clothes from your own closet, using yourself as a model with a full-length mirror or placing the clothes on a second-hand dress form (useful since garments on hangers are distorted, especially at the neckline). You can also practice drawing the people around you. Ask a friend or relative to hold still in a simple "balance-of-weight" pose for 5-minute sketches. The method shown on pages 13 to 17 can help improve your skill.

A great source for practice drawing is the pattern books that can be purchased from fabric shops at the end of each season. These books offer fashion drawings with fabric renderings, as well as photos you can work from. There are also flat drawings in which garment construction is stressed. One pattern book can offer a wide variety of poses, heads, hands, and feet (shoes). Also, a pattern book is an encyclopedia of garment detail.

Your collection of fashion drawings and photos should be expanded constantly. Current magazines will keep you aware of what is happening in the fashion world and aid in forecasting styles, fabrics, and colors that will soon be fashion. Consider as your teacher all published fashion art, past, present, and future.

Remember, you'll begin to find your own style by blatantly copying existing fashion drawings that you find appealing. (The exercises in this book mostly involve you in copying—crucial for beginners.) Don't hesitate to develop idols among the designers and illustrators whose work you admire. Go through the different periods of fashion history, taking bits here and pieces there. Eventually, you'll arrive at a style of your own. You should not expect to get there overnight. The freedom you hope to arrive at is based on early, meticulous detail work on *figure* (Part One of this book), *garments* (Part Two), and *fabrics* (Part Three).

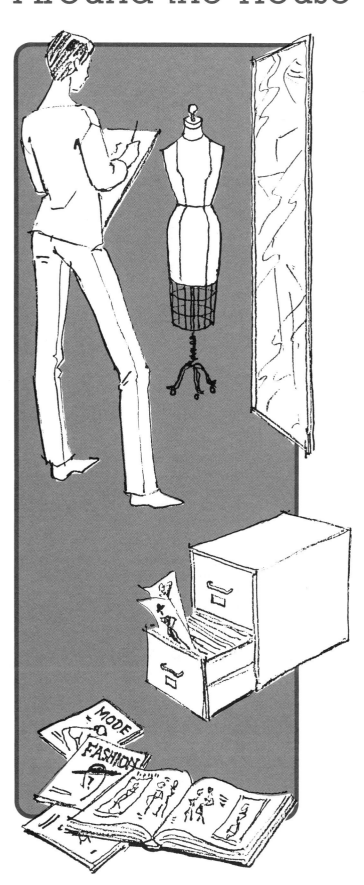

Light Source and Accent

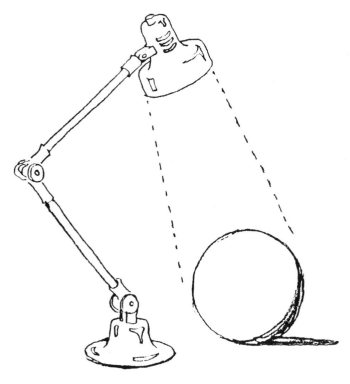

Accents (sharp, dark shadows) are placed to emphasize garment detail. For simplicity's sake, imagine that the light falling on the garment originates from one source, like the lamplight shining on the sphere above.

Assume that a light is shining on your fashion figure from an upper corner of the page. Such lighting results in dark accents within necklines and cuffs and under collars and lapels. Natural accents occur under bent arms, under hemlines, and along the unlighted side of the figure. Still other accents heighten the effect of folds and gathers. Finally, accents occur at all stress-fold lines of the garment.

Notice that in the unaccented line drawings at the near right, only the contours of the garment and figure indicate dimension. In the drawings to the far right, accents lend depth and realism.

With experience you can think of the light source and place the accents while creating the drawing.

Accents and Emphasis

In tracing garments over a croquis, you can use as destinations the various accents that result from the play of your imaginary light source on the garments. You can use these destinations—landmark accents, as it were—not only to draw to but as rest-and-plan stops. Remember, tracing over the croquis frees you to concentrate on garment proportion and detail. Drawing from destination to destination frees you to concentrate on the expressive quality of your line. Draw from left to right so as not to smear your drawings. If you are left-handed, draw from right to left.

Below are listed the accents which will serve to emphasize the folds, edges, and stress points of the belted turtleneck sweater and pants at left.

1. On either side of neck and under turtleneck collar encircling it
2. Stress marks at armpit; suggestion of bustline
3. Folds at bend in arm; residual folds on relaxed arm
4. Belt and folds it causes
5. Cuffs of garment curving around wrist
6. Under hemline of sweater
7. Stress folds at bent thigh and crotch
8. Stress folds from upper thigh and folds on weight-bearing leg
9. Stress folds radiating from bent knee
10. Under trousers cuff

You may have to make a number of tracings before the fashion look you want emerges. As you trace, refine and correct, always using the landmark accents as destinations. Concentrate on the line itself, which should be spontaneous and free yet economical and expressive. As you trace, try not lifting your pencil from the page too often. Just stop at each destination and plan ahead.

The landmark accents will change with different garment cuts. The illustrations that follow show a great variety of garments.

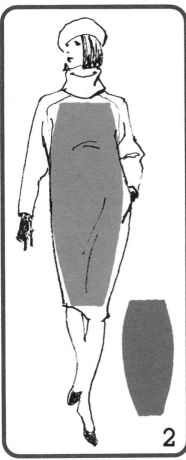

Garments as Simple Shapes

Learn to see each garment in terms of its shapes. If you are drawing from a fashion drawing, photo, or live model, keep the source far enough away so that you can see the entire stance and garment. Then squint to see the silhouette and dominant shapes.

After lightly indicating the pose (or using a croquis for a guide), draw the silhouette and dominant *shapes* of the garment. Place the drawing away from you to check for adjustments to ensure the accuracy of the garment's silhouette and proportions. *Finish* the drawing with details and accents.

The silhouettes shown are:

1. Spare, or "V"
2. Cocoon
3. Fitted, or hourglass
4. Oversized top, or "T"
5. Tent, or "A"

The Garment Dictates the Pose

The pose should show the garment to best advantage, focusing on the specific detail of a garment that sets it apart from all others.

On this page the shadow croquis show you where each garment touches, drapes on, or stands away from the body beneath it. Thus you can see how different poses are best for different garments:

1 The propped-leg pose is handy for culottes, gaucho, and other skirtlike pants.

2 If the major detail is confined to the back of a garment, a back view is appropriate but is usually accompanied by a front **vignette,** or partial drawing. (A vignette is also used when back detail accompanies a front view.)

3 The extreme ¾ view is commonly used to show both front and back detail.

4 The raised arm and ¾ view emphasize the full **dolman,** or batwing, sleeve; the blouson effect of the top; and the skirt slit, which the bent knee further displays.

Remember, you don't have to start from scratch with the pose for each garment. You can trace over a croquis.

Sequence
☐ Shirtwaist

The sequence you use when drawing a garment can greatly simplify the process. Following is a four-step approach to drawing a basic shirtwaist dress such as the one shown finished at the near right. This sequence can be used in drawing most garments with front closures.

1 It's usually best to draw the neckline, collar (if any), and front closure first to anchor the drawing. It will help your judgment as you do the sides, assisting you in keeping the figure slender. For the shirtwaist, begin by drawing the collar around the neck and down the front closure, overlapping the torso centerline (to the left, since this is a woman's garment; for men, overlap to the right). Draw the front placket to the belt and draw the belt around the waist. Add buttons on torso centerline. *Draw from destination to destination, using the arrows as guides.*

2 Working from top to bottom (so as not to smudge your drawing with your hand), draw the seams for the set-in sleeves. Next, draw the silhouette of the dress, showing the slight fullness blousing above and below the belt. Complete lower placket and buttons, and add tucks caused by the belt. Draw the fold created by the bent elbow, and draw cuffs around the wrists.

3 Next, connect the sleeves from shoulder seams to elbow folds and from elbow folds to cuffs. *Let destinations free you to think about the sleeve's fullness—how it might blouse.*

4 Complete with all the detail required to make a finished drawing. Here, finish with the figure's hair shape, face, and hands. With your finest line add garment details such as top stitching on collar placket and cuffs. For extra punch, add additional light-source accents.

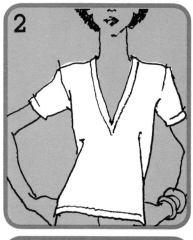

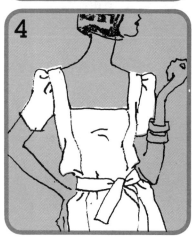

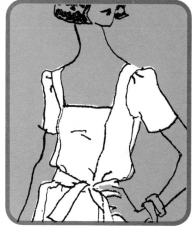

Necklines

☐ Front and Three-Quarter Views

Illustrated here is a sampling of basic necklines. A variety of sleeves and bodice styles are also shown and described. The examples are presented in both front and ¾ views to show the adjustments that must be made to accommodate the turned figure. The front view is used to show the shape with absolute accuracy. The turned view is designed to show more construction detail, for example, the side seam and the **arm's eye,** or round hole where the sleeve is attached to the body of the garment.

1 Sleeveless **jewel neckline** (plain round neckline at base of throat). Note bust **darts** (wedge-shaped tucks stitched out of garments to accommodate the contour of the body). In the ¾ view, shoulder and side seams are revealed.

2 V-neckline with short sleeves and easy fitting with no darts. In the ¾ view, the centerline has shifted and the shape of the neckline has changed.

3 **Scoop neck** (rounded and low cut) with short bishop sleeve (defined on page 73). **Princess line** (a fitted style established by vertical seams placed according to garment construction lines—which are often referred to as "princess lines"). The shift to ¾ view changes each aspect of the garment's appearance.

4 Square neckline, puffed sleeve and shoulder, princess line. (The princess line is used instead of darts.) Again, note the way the shift to the ¾ view alters the garment's appearance.

5 **Sweetheart neckline** (high in back, and low in front, where it is scalloped to resemble the top of a heart); **wing sleeves** (short, flared, gathered at the shoulders); princess line. Notice how the shape of the neckline subtly changes in the ¾ view.

6 **Draped neckline** with dolman sleeves. The drapery from the shoulders is expressed in different shapes in the ¾ view.

7 **Bateau (boat) neckline** (a wide neckline following the collarbone, high both front and back); an adaptation of **bishop sleeves** (long, full sleeves, usually gathered on a wristband, adapted from a bishop's robe). Note princess line starts at arm's eye instead of at shoulder seam. Three-quarter view reveals side seam and shoulder seam.

8 Wide V-neck; **cap sleeves** (very short sleeves); easy fitting so no darts necessary. Again, notice the way the shift to the ¾ view changes the placement of construction seams.

Necklines—like the collars on the next two pages—go around necks, which are cylinders with volume. Your previous study of contour lines will therefore help you to draw necklines and collars, not to mention bodice darts. Like necks, sleeves and arms are also cylinders, or tubes.

*In fact, all clothes are tubes. Unless you are rendering them in two dimensions (for a flat drawing), you will find yourself involved with **cylindrical perspective,** the representation of a cylindrical shape to convey an impression of three-dimensional space. A cross section of a cylindrical shape appears as an oval that recedes in depth. That is why the shape of a neckline changes subtly from the front view to the ¾ view.*

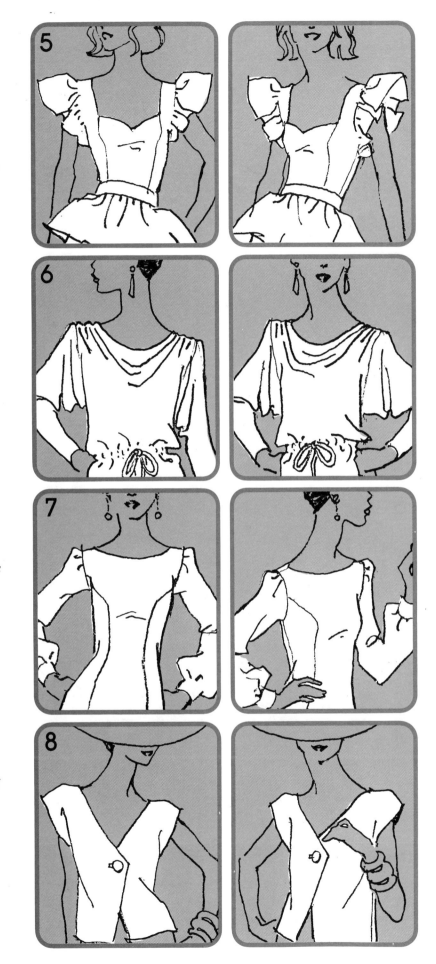

Collars and Sleeves

☐ Front and Three-Quarter Views

Collars are more complex than necklines. You must make sure they are drawn *around* the neck and to the appropriate scale. It takes a lot of practice. Illustrated here is a group of basic collars presented in both front and ¾ views to show the adjustment that must be made to accommodate the turned figure. The scale of the collar diminishes on the far side of the figure and seems larger on the near side—the effects of cylindrical perspective. Not only collars but sleeves and bodice styles are described below.

1 Man-tailored shirt collar; bust darts; cuffed, **set-in sleeves** (sleeves that are stitched inside an armhole cut in the front and back sections of a garment). The collar shown here is stitched onto a band (referred to as the "stand" of the collar) so that it stands up crisply. In the ¾ view, the shoulder and side seams are revealed.

2 Notched sport collar and short, set-in, cuffed sleeves; waist darts. Here, the collar is sewn, not to a band, but directly to the shirt body so that it lies flat when open. Again, in the ¾ view, side and shoulder seams are revealed.

3 Small, round **Peter Pan collar** and set-in puffed, cuffed sleeves. The fullness over the bust is in gathers from a shoulder yoke rather than darts. (A **yoke** is a horizontal division in a garment.) Observe how a ¾ view changes the silhouette of the garment.

4 Sailor collar and cuffed, short, set-in sleeves; bust darts. (The **sailor collar** is broad, with a square flap across the back tapering to a V in front. It is often worn with a tie and found on a **middy**, a loose overblouse.) The ¾ view exposes the back of the sailor collar.

5 **Mandarin collar** (stand-up slit band); **kimono sleeves** (full, wide, and long, kimono sleeves are often cut in one piece with the bodice, but these are set in with a **dropped shoulder line** extending beyond the top of the upper arm). In the ¾ view, the side and shoulder seams are revealed.

6 **Turtleneck** (high, close-fitting, turnover collar); **raglan sleeves** (extending from the neckline and so having slanted seams from the lowered underarm to the neck in front and back). The ¾ view reveals not only the side seam but the shoulder seam—continuous from the neck.

7 **Cowl neck** (modeled after a hooded garment, the cowl, formerly worn by monks) and set-in full bishop sleeves. Fullness from a yoke instead of darts. Notice how different the folds and falls of the garment appear in the ¾ view.

8 Ruffled V collar is **bias cut,** that is, cut diagonally across the grain of the fabric to fall more elegantly into folds. Bias detail cuff; bust darts. The shape of the neckline is adjusted to the ¾ view.

*To make the collars curve around the neck cylinders, start drawing from the back of each collar, following the curve of the neckline in an arc. Then draw the opening shape, or **roll.** As most collars are symmetrical—the same on both sides of the garment—your drawing will reflect this by giving both sides equal detail.*

When you have mastered the drawing of symmetrical collars, look in your fashion files for asymmetrical collars, different on each side of the garment. The front pose is chosen for asymmetrical designs.

Remember, the collar can be an important part of the fashion statement a garment makes. Its type and size are very much determined by fashion cycles. Consequently, collars must be drawn with attention to shape and scale.

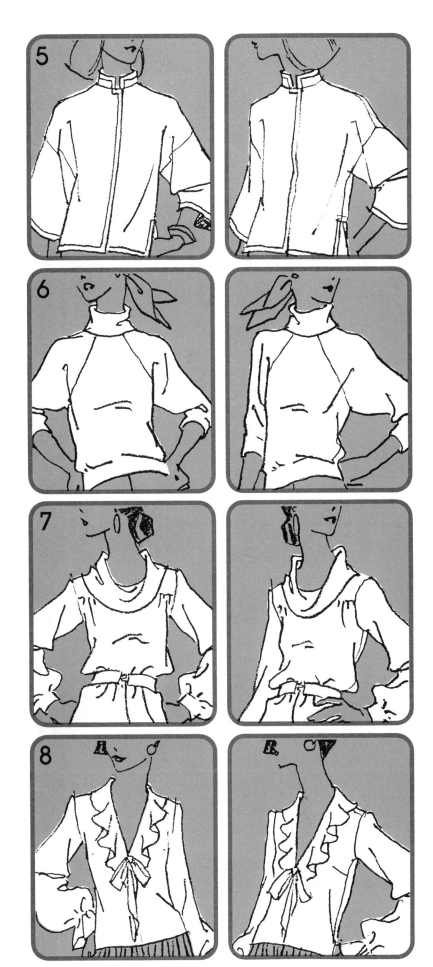

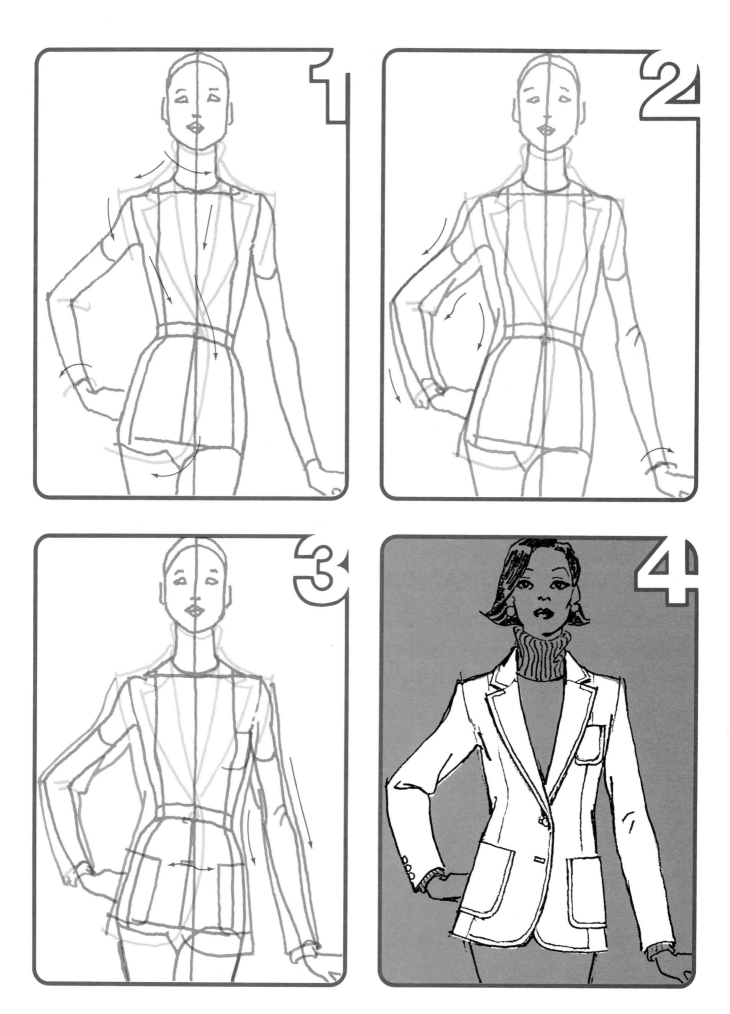

The Woman's Blazer

The blazer jacket has been an important woman's wardrobe item for many decades. The silhouette alters as fashion dictates, but the *concept* remains essentially the same. The sequence used for the shirtwaist applies to the blazer because, like so many other garments, it has a center front closure. Remember garments curve around the figure, and should be drawn in the direction of the arrows.

1 Begin by anchoring your drawing with the turtleneck circling the neck; then draw the edge of the front closure. Add the notched lapel on one side and match it on the other; then draw the slightly extended shoulders, indicating the seams to which the sleeves will be attached. Draw the elbow fold accents and curved cuffline of the bent arm as destinations for drawing the left sleeve. Finally, add the button on the centerline at the waist.

2 Draw the left side of the blazer from the sleeve seam to the hemline. Note how the line changes direction just above the waistline. Finish the left sleeve, drawing to the elbow folds. (A fold of fabric may fall from the direction of the shoulder and join the elbow folds.) To aid you in drawing the right sleeve, place accent marks at the elbow folds and then draw the curve of the cuff.

3 Draw the right side of the body of the garment, eased from the figure, before drawing the right sleeve. A break in the line of the sleeve's underside will soften the effect. Then add buttonholes and pockets. Note how the top edges of the pockets are in line with the lower buttonhole.

4 Finish with details such as the pockets, sleeve buttons, vertical darts, buttonholes, and **top stitching** (the fine line of visible stitching paralleling the outline of the lapels, front and pockets). Light-source accents will add punch to the drawing.

The classic blazer sequences above will help you draw not only the variations at right but the four jackets illustrated on the next page.

Shorter, more fitted blazer with puffed sleeves. Note slit pockets, single button, top stitching on lapels.

Double-breasted boxy blazer (less fitted). Note the indication of double **venting** (opening at the bottom seams of the blazer's back).

Jackets/ Suits

Chanel suit—A timeless classic first created by French designer Coco Chanel in 1927. Note braid trim.

Bolero jacket—Short and fitted (note how princess line is one seam from the arm's eye). Not all boleros are collarless.

Cardigan jacket—This style is always collarless. The example here is single-breasted with shoulder darts on the sleeves.

Tie-wrap suit—No front closure other than a tie-belt. This example has a notched collar and patch pockets.

The jacket styles shown at the left occur time and again in fashion cycles. Although the true Chanel suit is skirted, all these jackets can combine with either skirts or pants to make suits or **separates** outfits. On the following pages, you will be learning to draw a variety of skirts and pants. For now, concentrate on the jackets shown here and from your fashion files.

The suits and jackets at the left are drawn in a sequence of steps roughly similar to the one you just learned for the classic blazer. Always begin drawing a jacket by working around the neck and down the front closure.

The fit of jackets fluctuates with fashion. From season to season, be alert to subtle differences of silhouette. The size of a lapel can date a jacket; so can the shape of the shoulders, the length of the jacket, the sleeve styling, and the pocket styling. Careful attention is necessary to capture the fashion flair of each jacket.

To study their details, try hanging some jackets on hangers or a dress form. Try them on and sketch your reflection in a full-length mirror. Or ask a friend to model for you. At first, make jacket details clear and realistic. Later, to create fashion effect, you can practice exaggerating the major features.

If you are sketching a jacket from a model, be sure to edit wrinkles but keep the stress marks and folds that occur at structurally meaningful points such as the bend of the elbow.

Skirts

The skirt is an independent clothing item or—when attached to a bodice—the lower portion of a dress. It is a tube with an ellipse at the top (waistline) and one at the bottom (hemline). When you draw a skirt, be sure these two ellipses are tilted with the hips, so an equal amount of fabric goes from waistline to hemline on both sides.

The silhouette of the skirt alters with fashion cycles and is determined by the basic construction. Four types of skirt are shown at right: the A-line, the dirndl, the gored, and the gathered. We will be using the four types to study basic techniques.

Study the silhouette of each skirt. Within the fuller skirts the columns of fullness echo the shape of the silhouette. The *amount* of fullness is indicated by the number of columns and the depth of the folds showing at the hemline. The *fall* of the columns of fullness is affected by the stance of the figure but depends primarily on the cut of the garment, which dictates whether columns fall from waist, hip, thigh, or knee.

The **A-line skirt** is the simplest of the four basic skirts. The slight fullness falls from the hips and is usually darted from the waistband to ensure a smooth fit. The **dirndl** has fullness created by the gathers from the waistband. The dirndl varies in fullness and becomes eventually the **gathered skirt**. The **gored skirt** is sewn from flaring shapes to fit smoothly from the waistband. The columns of fullness fall from the hips.

In each sequence on the following pages, a dotted line designates the hemline ellipse; arrows indicate the direction the silhouette lines are to be drawn. The dirndl and the A-line are simple silhouettes and can be drawn in two steps. The gored and gathered skirts require three steps because they contain shapes within shapes.

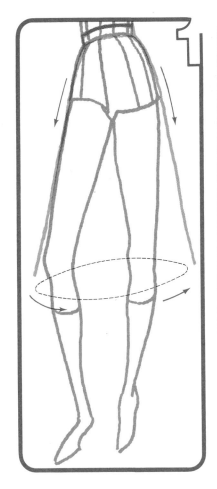

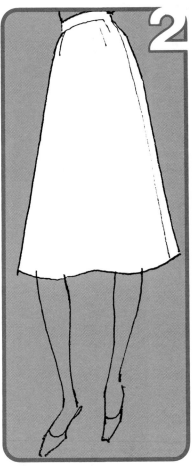

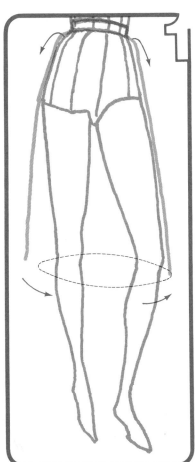

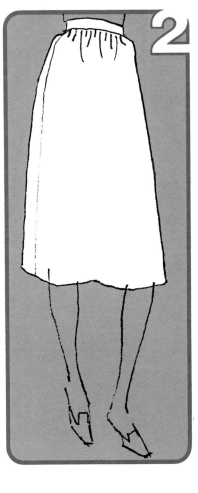

Basic Skirts

A-Line

1 Over a suitably posed croquis, draw the silhouette, tilting the waistband and *lightly indicated* hemline ellipse with the hips.

2 Draw the hemline eased to accommodate the bent leg and to suggest fabrication; then finish with waist darts. Add a side seam if warranted by the pose.

Dirndl

1 When drawing the silhouette, note the slight puff created by the gathers. Tilt the waistband and hemline ellipse with the hips.

2 Ease the hemline to accommodate the bent leg and to suggest fabric. Finish with gathers irregular in length and direction. Add a side seam if the pose warrants.

Gored

1 Draw the silhouette flared from the hips. Tilt the waistband and hemline ellipse with the hips. Within the silhouette, add flared columns of fullness.

2 Draw the hemline on the columns of fullness; then draw the hemline between the columns.

3 Finish by drawing the gore seams. (These may become lost in the folds descending toward the hem.)

Gathered

1 As always, the waistband and hemline ellipse are tilted with the hips. Draw the silhouette gathered from the waistband; then draw the columns of fullness with irregular widths.

2 First draw the hemline on the columns of fullness and then between the columns.

3 Complete by adding irregular gathers from the waistband.

Layered Skirts

Flounced

Each **flounce** (layer) of the skirt shown at upper right can be treated as a short, gathered skirt. The flounces are attached in overlapping "shingles" to a foundation—here, a gored skirt. The process here is for a low-waisted skirt:

1 Lightly draw the shape of the foundation skirt. The waistband and the hemline ellipse of each flounce are tilted with the hips. Starting at the top, draw short columns of fullness, irregular in width and position, to create an overlapping silhouette. Finish the hemline of each flounce as for an individual gathered skirt.

2 Complete the columns of fullness.

3 Finish by carefully erasing construction lines and adding irregular gathers at the flounce tops.

Tiered

The skirt shown at lower right is based on the gathered skirt. Rather than being sewn to a foundation skirt, each layer, or **tier,** is sewn to the bottom edge of the one above and is affected by the columns of fullness falling from waistband to hem.

1 Lightly draw the silhouette and columns of fullness as though for a gathered skirt.

2 Draw the waistband tilted with the hips; lightly indicate the ellipse for the bottom of each tier and the hemline. (The tier seams echo the hem.)

3 Alter the silhouette and columns of fullness by indicating gather shapes at the top of each tier. Finish by erasing obvious construction lines and adding irregular gathers from the top of each tier.

Pleated Skirts

Knife Pleats

The **knife pleat** can vary in width according to the skirt's design. It folds on itself in one direction. Like other pleats, these open as they approach the hemline, which is tricky to draw: The angle of the ellipse must always be observed while each pleat is drawn individually.

1 Draw the silhouette, tilting the waistband and hemline ellipse with the hips. Establish a centerline from waistband to hips as a guide for drawing the pleats flaring from hips to hem. Work center to left, then center to right. Space the pleats equally at center source and even closer approaching each side. The width may vary at the hemline to accommodate the pose.

2 Finish by angling the hemline on each pleat to suggest depth.

3 The results should look like this.

Accordian Pleats

Shallower than knife pleats, **accordian pleats** are also closer together—there are *more* of them and the resulting skirt is fuller.

1 Begin by lightly planning the columns of fullness and the hemline of a gored skirt. Tilt the waistband and hemline with the hips as you draw a gored-skirt silhouette. From waistband to hem draw a bold guideline centered on the columns of fullness. Starting with the center column, draw vertical lines from waistband to hem on each column. Some lines will be lost in the overlap of columns; others will start on the edge of columns.

2 Finish the hemline with slanted lines for each pleat. Starting with the center column, "hem" the columns themselves before the spaces between, slanting the hemline toward the center from either side for the look of gored fullness.

3 The results should look like this.

More Pleats

Engineered Pleats

Engineered pleats are as varied as designers' inventions. The skirt shown here is not, strictly speaking, a pleated skirt, but rather a skirt with engineered pleats added for detail. The front panel of this skirt has knife pleats on either side.

1 Lightly draw an A-line silhouette, tilting the waistband and hemline ellipse with the hips. Align the panel with the centerline of the figure; then add vertical lines for the pleats, flaring slightly from waistband to hem.

2 Finish the panel with a sharp hemline, and angle the pleats. The balance of the skirt curves around the figure.

3 The results should look like this.

Box Pleats

Made by forming two folded edges, one facing right and the other left, each **box pleat** has an **inverted pleat** on its reverse. In this example the pleats are sewn down and released from the hips. Depending on the pose, indentions between the boxes may vary, although the boxes stay the same.

1 Draw an A-line silhouette, the waistband, and the hemline ellipse. Then draw the hip area where the sewn-down pleats are released. From each sewn-down seam, draw the upside-down released lines of the pleats, working out from the center of the skirt.

2 Begin drawing the boxes on the hemline and in their indentations. Keep the edges sharp.

3 Finish drawing the boxes and indentations on the hemlines. As the pleats fall open, a third vertical line and an added hem indication may be needed.

Very Full Skirts

Gored and Gathered

The combination of gores and gathers produces maximum fullness. The **gored-and-gathered skirt** is best shown with movement.

1 Draw the silhouette and tilt the waistband and hemline ellipse with the hips. Draw irregular-width columns of fullness from the waist, flaring to the hem.

2 Start drawing the hemline on the columns of fullness. (The hemline on the recessed planes of fullness will appear shorter.)

3 Add gathers and gore seams. Lines used for gathers are irregular in length and placement. Lines used for gores can disappear into the columns.

Unpressed Pleats

The skirt with **unpressed pleats** is structured from the waistband, relaxing into a loose hemline. Here, sewn-down pleats release from the hips.

1 Draw the silhouette and tilt the waistband and hemline ellipse with the hips. Space the sewn-down pleats evenly over the hips. Draw the columns of fullness with upside-down uneven V's. Let some lines reach the hemline.

2 Begin the hemline following the general ellipse, but let it wave enough to suggest the fullness and construction of the skirt. Treat the columns of fullness individually.

3 Complete the hemline. It should fall in rounded folds rather than sharp ones.

Divided Skirts

Skirts divided into two pant legs are known as **divided skirts.** Of these, there are two principal kinds, gaucho pants and culottes, with many possible variations on each.

Gaucho Pants

The simplest divided skirt is the midcalf **gaucho pant,** originally worn by Argentine cowboys. This example employs darts from the waistband for fit over the hip. Other styles might use gathers or pleats.

1 Draw the waistband and tilt the lightly indicated hemline ellipse with the hips. This silhouette is much like that of the A-line skirt.

2 Complete the silhouette and draw the center seam from waistband to crotch. Draw the diagonal stress mark at the end of the center seam and indicate the division of the skirt into two "legs."

3 Finish by adding the individual hemlines, side seam, inseam, and stress marks as shown.

Culottes

This divided skirt is characterized by the gathers of fullness or pleats used to disguise the division into legs and to suggest a conventional skirt. In the **culottes** shown here, the division into legs is disguised by a mock pleat from waist to hem.

1 Draw the waistband and tilt the lightly indicated hemline with the hips. Draw the A-line silhouette and angle the box pleat with the hips.

2 Draw the individual hemlines on either side of the box pleat. Indicate the pant leg as seen through the mock box pleat. (If the spread of the stance were wider, both pant legs would be shown.)

3 Finish by adding the small released pleats from the waistband providing fit over the hips.

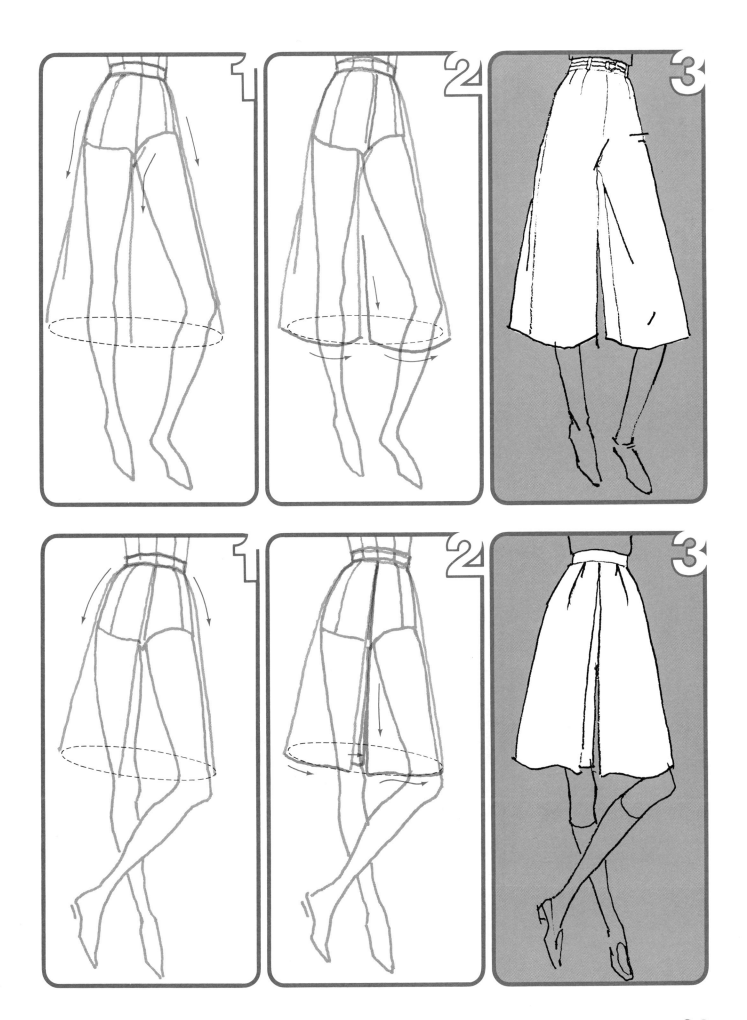

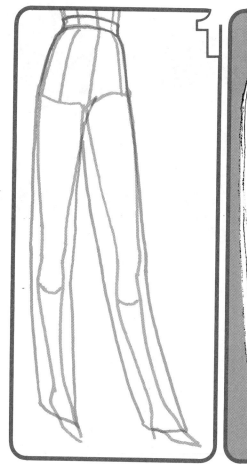

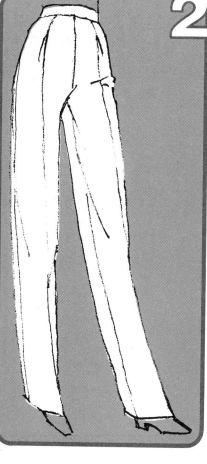

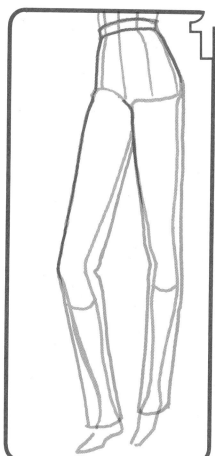

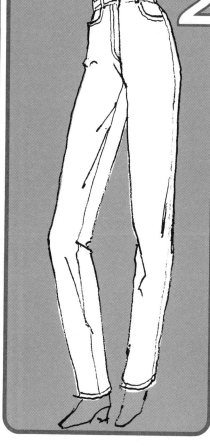

Pants

Current fashion includes a wide variety of pant silhouettes. The process drawings on this page teach you a very basic slack shape and a typical designer-jean look.

Slacks with Pressed Crease

1 Tilt the waistband with the hips. Draw the silhouette fitted on the hip and falling to the hem on the weight-bearing leg. A slight indentation below the knee relaxes the line. The pant will rest against the front of the extended leg and fall away behind. Tilt the center seam with the hips, adding the diagonal crease at the crotch.

2 Draw sewn-down and released pleats from waistband and pressed creases as shown. Draw hemlines slanted toward the pressed creases. Add seam and stress folds.

Jeans

1 Use the approach described above but fit the pant closer to the leg. There is a break line behind the bent knee, and stress folds radiate from the kneecap.

2 Add the belt loops, pockets, and fly front. Add top stitching.

Variations

Using the steps given for the classic pants shown at left, you should be able to draw the variations shown at right and other variations, such as shorts of different lengths.

1. Above-the-knee cuffed pants
2. Tight capri pants
3. Very draped pants
4. Gathered-front knickers
5. Pegged-hemline pants
6. Above-the-ankle pirate pants

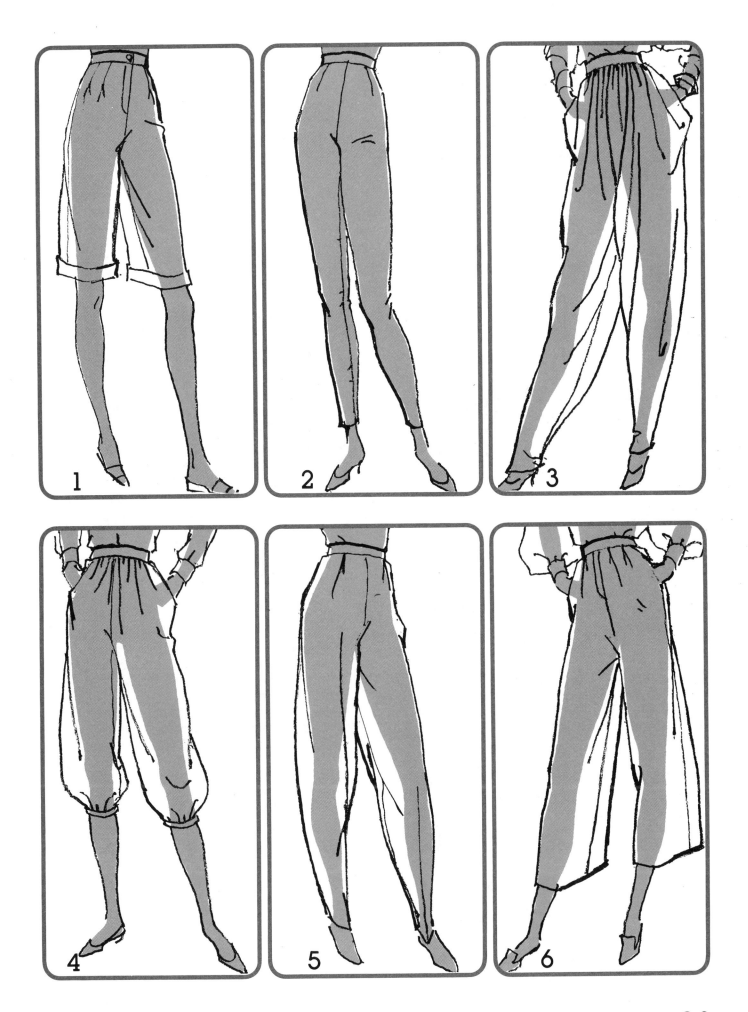

Accent and Emphasis

Below is a list of suggested accents to emphasize folds, edges, and stress points of male garments. Though the example at left shows accents for a casual open-neck shirt and jeans, the way the accents were used can be applied to other male garments as well.

Remember, the drawing of garments on male figures expresses a different *attitude* than the drawing of garments on female figures. A bold, vigorous line quality gives a fashion drawing a masculine tone. Although men's fashions change more slowly and subtly than those of women, the details and fit of male apparel are very important.

Use the light-source technique explained on page 67. After you have studied the way accents were used to draw the garments on this page, move on to draw the garments shown with shadow croquis on the pages that follow. Note how the body beneath the clothing is revealed in the shadow croquis; note where the garments rest on the body and where they fall away from it.

Accents

1. On either side of neck; under collar
2. At armpits; under pocket flaps; at meeting of front closure
3. Bend of arm folds
4. Belt; folds caused by belt
5. Cuff curved around arm
6. Stress folds at crotch, bent thigh
7. Residual folds at weight-bearing knee
8. Stress mark radiating from bent knee to inseam and behind-knee folds
9. Break of trousers at shoe
10. Under hemline of trousers

Men's Casual Wear with Shadow Croquis

The shadow croquis are showing the body under the garments. Wherever the garment rests on the body there can be stress on the fabric. Even though the body does not show on the final drawing, its stance affects the silhouette.

1 Polo shirt (sweater tied over shoulders), pleated cotton trousers

2 Jumpsuit with elasticized waist inserts, pant legs bloused into boots

3 Windbreaker, crew-neck sweater over casual slacks.

Active Sportswear with Shadow Croquis

Again, shadow croquis show the bodies under the garments that would ordinarily obscure them. It is important, especially when drawing loose clothes, to consider the shape of the body beneath them.

1 Top, shorts, sweatband, athletic socks, and sport shoes (soccer)

2 Zippered hooded sweater shirt, shorts (après racquetball)

3 Hooded slicker, slipover, rolled ducks (sailing)

Menswear with Shadow Croquis

The shadow croquis show you where the garments touch the figures and fall away from them.

1 *Natural-shoulder suit:* Slightly sloping natural shoulders revealed by lack of structure; somewhat boxy jacket.

2 *Three-piece suit:* Some padding in the shoulders; darts placed to slightly shape waist.

3 *Sports jacket with sweater and slacks:* Notice the stress points where the clothes touch the body.

The Man's Blazer

The blazer is important in any man's wardrobe. Tailoring variations occur slightly from season to season, but the basic garment remains the same. What's really important about menswear is the fit.

The technique used to draw the blazer applies equally to suits, sport coats, and other outerwear. The process example at left is a two-button jacket with patch pockets with flaps. At right are two variations on the basic-blazer theme. To reproduce either the blazer or the variations, draw from point to point, following the arrows and using folds and stress marks as destinations.

1 Again, anchor your drawing by rounding the neck with the collar of the shirt. Next, draw the edge of the front closure on the left side of the garment. Starting at the neckline, cross the centerline at the waist and curve into the hemline. In drawing the right front-closure edge, make sure it meets the left side at the centerline. Now add the collar and notched lapels. Draw the slightly extended shoulders sloping to the seams of the arm's eye; then indicate the curved cuffs and the elbow folds as destinations for drawing the left sleeve. Draw the upper part of the left sleeve from shoulder and armpit to elbow folds. Add the button on the centerline and the necktie.

2 Complete the jacket by drawing from the arm's eye to the hem, with a slight fit at the waist, as shown. Note that the lower part of the sleeve rests on the forearm.

3 Complete the right sleeve, indicating some fullness at the elbow; then draw the pockets. Add the shirt cuffs.

4 Carefully draw the details using your finest line: vertical dart, buttonholes, top stitching, and sleeve buttons.

Double-breasted blazer with pocket flaps, eased silhouette, and peaked lapels.

Continental-cut jacket featuring pointed, closely fitted peaked shoulderline; high-cut armholes; fitted and flared silhouette.

Gallery of Dresses

The gallery of dresses and the galleries that follow will expose you to a wide variety of silhouettes and introduce you to a great many terms of the trade. The galleries will also give you a smattering of fashion history. Pay close attention to the fashion cycles that occur and reoccur. Some of the items in each gallery are timeless classics; others are definitely period pieces. All are twentieth-century fashions.

1. Natural waistline, early '50s
2. Dropped waistline, early '20s
3. High waistline, early '60s
4. Darted waistline, early '50s
5. Chemise, late '50s
6. Trapeze, late '50s
7. Shift, early '60s
8. Coat dress, late '30s
9. Tent dress, early '70s
10. Tunic dress, early teens
11. Handkerchief hemline, late '20s
12. Empire, late '50s
13. Strapless with peplum, late '40s
14. Bias cut, early '30s

As you move through these galleries, study the hands, feet, and accessories as well as the garments. Note that shoes, gloves, handbags, and jewelry compliment the garments and help in creating the total fashion look. Notice that each figure not only presents a total fashion look but tells a fashion story. As you draw, keep an image in mind. Ask yourself questions like, Who would wear this garment? How would she wear and accessorize it? Where would she wear it? Tell yourself a short story about each fashion figure, and you can express more life and excitement in the drawing.

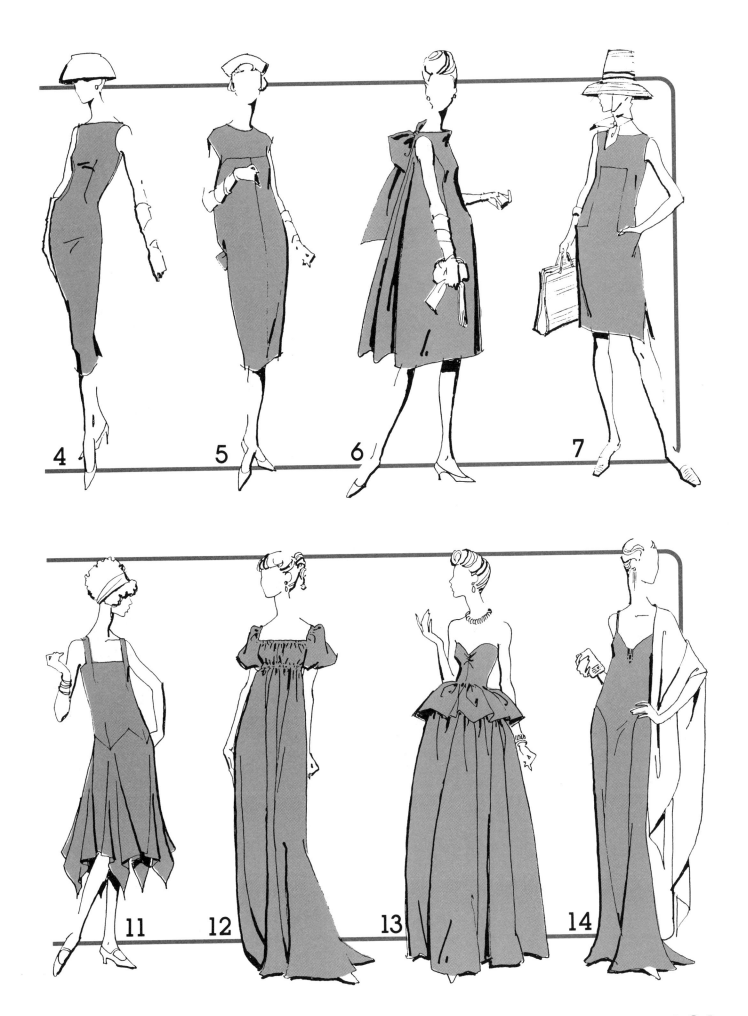

Gallery of Suits

1. Chanel suit, late-'50s version of a classic design
2. Fur-trimmed suit, late teens
3. Mini-skirt suit, early '70s
4. Tailored suit, early '40s
5. Dinner suit, early '80s
6. Double-breasted suit, early '60s
7. Shawl-collared suit, late '20s

Gallery of Coats

1. Trench coat, early '80s
2. Swagger coat, late '30s
3. Maxi coat, late '60s
4. Chesterfield coat, early '40s
5. Polo coat, early '30s
6. Double-breasted coat, early '60s
7. Greatcoat, early '20s

Coats are tailored garments, like suits and blazers, but constructed in heavier fabrics. Style details such as lapels, pockets, flaps, and top stitching may be drawn in larger scale to balance the coat's larger volume. Accessories help indicate the season in which the coat is intended to be worn.

Gallery of Women's Pants and Tops

1. Capri shirt and pants, late '50s
2. Beach pajamas, early '30s
3. Pedal pushers, shell, '50s
4. Hot pants, pirate shirt, early '70s
5. Flares and sweater, '70s
6. Knickers, jacket, early '80s
7. Slack suit, early '40s
8. Designer jeans, western shirt, late '70s
9. Patio pants, bandeau, late '60s
10. Bell-bottoms, slipover, late '60s
11. Baggy pants, padded shoulder blouse, late '70s
12. Stretch stirrup pants, over-blouse, late '50s
13. Jodhpurs, late '20s
14. Hip-huggers, late '60s

Note that the hairstyles, hats, and accessories reflect the look of the specific period from which they have been resurrected.

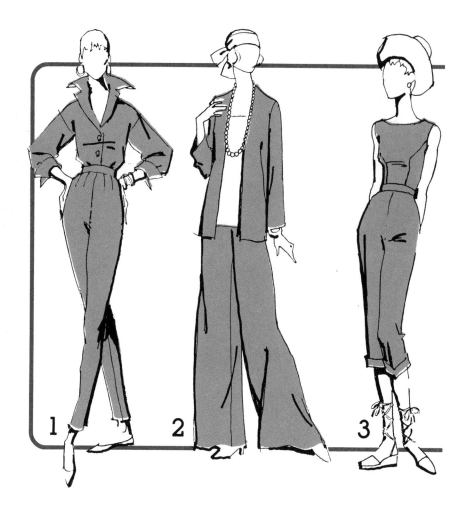

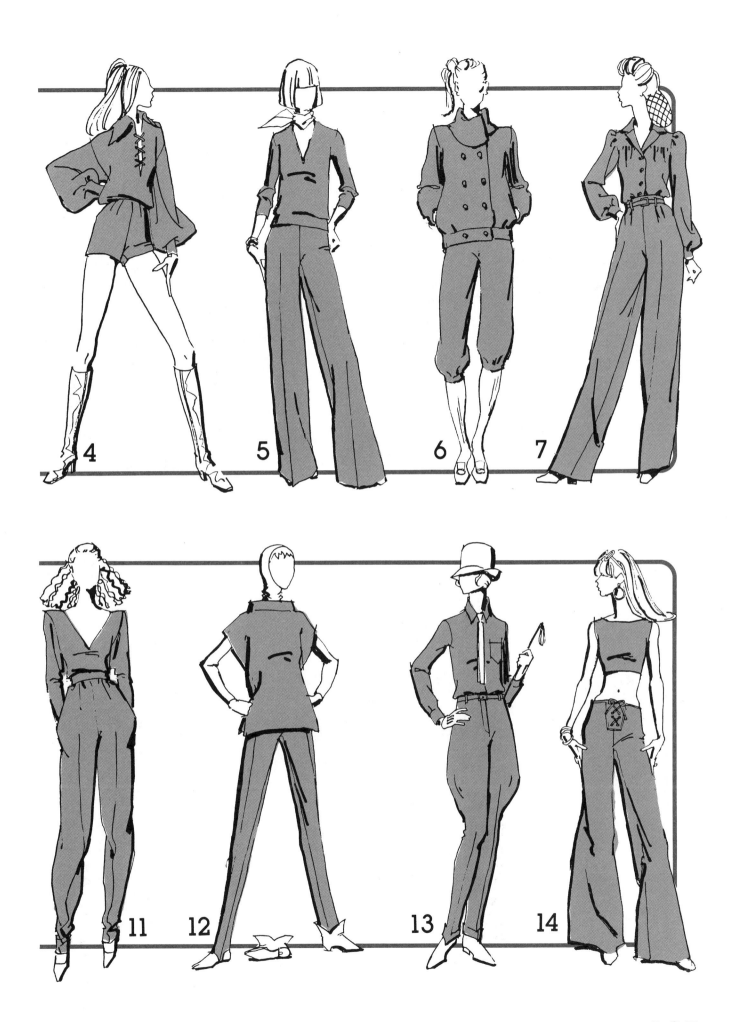

Gallery of Men's Suits

As with the women's fashions, the galleries of men's fashions contain both classics and period pieces. Men's fashions change more slowly and subtly than those of women. The fashion look is established by the exact width of a shoulder, lapel, or tie. The silhouette and current fit of a suit are crucial.

1. Tuxedo ("black tie"), '20s
2. Morning suit, classic
3. Formal attire (top hat and "tails"), classic
4. Three-piece suit, '70s
5. Mod suit, late '60s
6. Continental suit, late '50s
7. Zoot suit, early '40s

Gallery of Men's Sportswear

The following examples are all contemporary, except for No. 7

1. Western gear
2. Jogging top, pants
3. Tennis shorts, sweater
4. Ski suit, cap
5. Polo togs, classic
6. Hiking shorts with boots and backpack
7. Plus-four knickers with sweater, cap, circa 1920

One of the strongest influences in men's sportswear in recent years has been the military. (It gave us the T-shirt, bomber jacket, and jumpsuit in World War II.) Other major influences have been active sports and, of course, western gear.

Gallery of Adolescents

Unlike the adult's galleries, the adolescents' and younger children's galleries contain only contemporary garments. Because of the endless variations of garments favored by these age groups, the examples illustrated here are limited. However, they do reflect the wide range and diversity of the school and sportswear styles available. Passing fads have been ignored.

1. Athletic jacket, khakis
2. Sweater, fly-front pants
3. Down-filled vest, jeans
4. Knit cap, bulky sweater, pants, leg warmers
5. Polo shirt, shorts
6. Western shirt, jeans
7. Sweater set, box-pleated skirt, ribbed hose

Gallery of Big Kids

These examples contain a mixture of play, school, and dress clothes.

1. Long, flounced dress, ruffle detail
2. Lace-trimmed blouse, prairie skirt
3. T-shirt, warm-up pants
4. Ruffle-trimmed blouse, cummerbund, gathered skirt
5. Middy blouse, pleated skirt, tights
6. Crewneck sweater, slacks
7. Rugby shirt, jeans

When drawing children, you may want to create a situation or story for each fashion figure, as was suggested for drawing adults.

Gallery of Toddlers and Little Kids

These are mostly play clothes, with a few dress clothes.

1. Turtleneck under long coveralls with buttoned crotch
2. Shirred yoke dress, matching panties
3. T-shirt under short coveralls with buttoned crotch
4. Knit hooded top with zipper-front closure, knit pants
5. Ruffle-trimmed pinafore over dress
6. Knit cap, turtleneck sweater, knife-pleated skirt, tights
7. Middy top, short pants, knee-length socks
8. T-shirt under long coveralls
9. T-shirt, long pants with suspenders
10. Hat, pleated-back coat, tights

Accessories
☐ Hats and Scarves

Parts Two and Three show many examples of accessories—hats, bags, scarves, belts, and jewelry. Now we're again concerned with specifics. Hats, fitted to the head, and scarves, arranged around the neck, present two of the more difficult challenges in the successful addition of accessories.

Provided here are examples that will aid in drawing these and most other styles. They are, from top to bottom, a snap-brimmed hat, a rolled-brimmed hat, a beret, and a man's western-type hat. The following steps work for all examples.

1 Draw the head and indicate the features and hair. Place the hatband line. Block in the scarf shapes, being sure the scarf circles the neck.

2 Draw the crown and brim of the hat. (Keep in mind that shape and scale are important. Note that some hats fit the head closely; others have raised crowns.) See how the scarf's contour changes from a basic shape to a fabric as the line is refined.

3 Complete the hat with trim and erase any guidelines. The scarf is completed with folds and carefully drawn knots (if appropriate). Be sure to indicate gathered folds where the ends of the scarf pass through the knots.

Hats are infinite in their variety, but the approach I've shown will help with most styles. The approach given for scarves will also help you draw most varieties of scarves. Again, I suggest that you refer to your files of fashion scrap when you require a specific accessory.

Fashion Photo as a Model

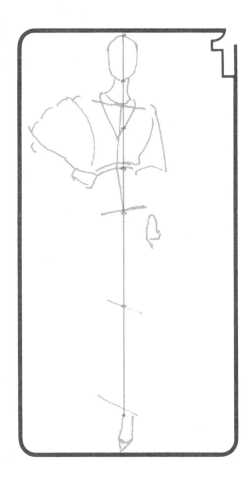

This exercise is designed to translate a fashion photo into a drawing of fashion proportions. Photography adds weight to the subject, so that even the slender, leggy fashion model appears shorter and heavier than the ideal fashion drawing. The goal is to stretch the figure to the ideal.

In the steps shown here the method used is a direct plan-as-you-go technique. If you feel the need, you may analyze the pose and draw a croquis over which to work, but it is not absolutely necessary to work from a croquis when drawing from a source such as a photo, an existing illustration, or a live model.

1 Plan the figure on the page, using the balance-of-weight formula. Draw and mark the plumb line for vertical proportions. Lightly indicate head, neck, and the weight-bearing foot. Add slightly tilted ribcage top (collarbone). Lightly indicate tilted waistline and draw relaxed torso centerline. Think ahead. Visualize the figure

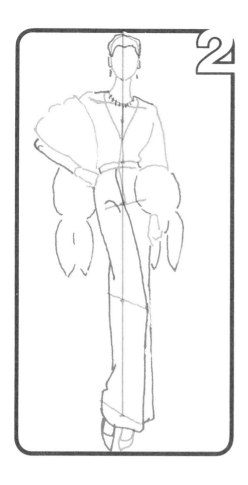

on the page. Estimate and mark drawing destinations as indicated: the head, neck, neckline, shoulder width, and tilted waistband. Place the hands and weight-bearing foot. Now start drawing the major shapes such as the bodice and, in this case, the furs.

2 Complete the fur and skirt shapes. Place the relaxed foot. Starting with the line of the bent knee, begin to indicate the gathers from the waistband.

3 Finish the gathers from the waistband on the skirt, bodice, and from the shoulders. Add facial features, hair and construction details, as well as folds and stress marks. If necessary, retrace your initial drawing rather than attempting to clean it up with unattractive erasures.

The drawing on this page is the fourth draft of the photograph, which was furnished by the Celanese Corporation. Note that the hairstyle was changed in the drawing.

Fashion Illustration as a Practice Model

Practicing from a favorite fashion illustration offers many benefits. The original illustrator has already translated the figure into a fashion image. The stance has been exaggerated and unnecessary folds have been eliminated. The important folds and accents are readily apparent. Details to be emphasized have already been selected, and a fashion look has been established.

This drawing by noted fashion illustrator Richard Holiman was furnished by Neiman-Marcus.

1 Using the balance-of-weight formula, draw and mark the plumb line for vertical proportions. Lightly indicate head, neck, and collarbone tilt. Draw the relaxed torso centerline and the hip tilt. Now stop to plan. Visualize the figure on the page. Mark the drawing destinations. Lightly draw the neckline, the front closure with button, the bodice and sleeve shapes, and the tilted waistband. Start drawing the skirt with the center columns of fullness. Then place the weight-bearing foot and draw the leg to it. Add the relaxed foot and leg. The

elbow and bracelet are good drawing destinations. Note that the hand placed high on the waistline forces the shoulder to an exaggerated tilt.

2 Now add bodice detail, epaulets, pockets, and stitching. Complete the skirt with columns of fullness and silhouette.

3 Finish by accenting your light planning line with bolder strokes. Add facial features and accessories. With your kneaded eraser pick out any construction lines that were not absorbed by the stronger lines or trace a fresh draft of the drawing.

Remember this is a copycat drawing for your instruction and is *not* to be included in your portfolio.

Your files of scrap should contain drawings of many illustrators and designers. Working from your favorites will help you develop the look you want to call your style. Try to emulate the artist's style by analyzing the technique used to achieve it. Be like the apprentice fine artist working from a masterpiece.

Drawing from a Live Model

Practicing from a live model is an excellent exercise for developing the skills required to create swift, detailed, accurate drawings. I believe that a five-minute pose offers enough time to draw the major shapes of the stance and is not too taxing for the model, although other teachers suggest shorter poses for experienced students and longer ones for beginners. *Anyone can model for the fashion figure.*

Begin this exercise with pencil but switch to a fine marker for Step 2.

1 Have the model assume a relaxed, natural pose. With your pencil, lightly draw the plumb line for vertical proportions. Establish basic shapes and indicate key destinations as in drawing from a photo or fashion drawing.

2 Now switch to a marker. It will save you eraser time and increase your concentration and selection as you draw from point to point and refine basic shapes. The trick is to retain fashion proportions while drawing from the model's hair shapes, garments, and stance.

3 *Select* and add necessary folds and stress marks to the drawing. (File them in your head for reference when drawing without a model.) Finish the drawing with an appropriate amount of construction seams and other details. Study and, if needed, memorize any fine details that have not been included in the five-minute time span so you can complete them after the model steps down.

The five-minute live model drawing forces you to observe and make quick decisions. This exercise is not easy, so plan to practice it over and over. The examples here were drawn by my students in five minutes using fellow students as models. See page ii for the students' names.

Phoebe

Part Three
Rendering the Fabrics

Skill at rendering specific fabrics is useful for the designer and mandatory for the illustrator. With the finished garment in mind, the designer uses fabric indication, reinforced by notes and fabric swatches, to present a complete visual concept of the garment. The illustrator produces drawings of existing garments that must clearly express the cut, silhouette, and fabric detail to entice buyers.

To render a finished fashion drawing, the pattern, texture, and "hand," or feel, of the fabric are required. For this, line quality is of paramount importance. The lines used to describe, for example, a soft jersey differ dramatically from those used to describe a crisp cotton (see pages 120–123).

After line quality, accurate depiction of pattern is the next step in suggesting specific fabrics. From very controlled stripes, checks, plaids, and geometrics to the looser floral and abstract designs, placement, scale, and color tone must be taken into account.

Full color is also a consideration. Part Three opens with a full-color introduction to marker coloration on a number of fabrics and instructions on how to reproduce them. The exercises following the color introduction lead you from the most basic patterns through increasingly complex challenges, not only of pattern but also of texture. The skills shown in Part Three will prepare you for almost any fabric.

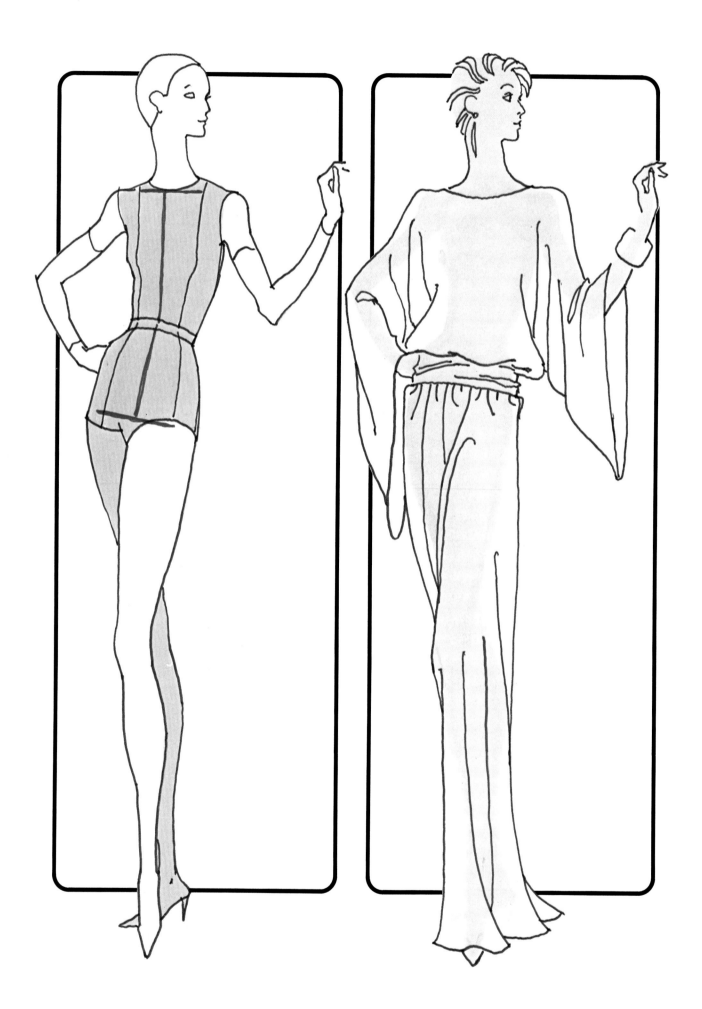

Border Print

Though most advertising and editorial fashion illustration is done in black, white, and tones between, more illustrators are working in full color than ever before. With the introduction of color markers, designers now have a quick color tool for indicating solids, patterns, and trims. In the past, water soluble paints were used for color. They are still favored by illustrators and designers who are skilled in their use and take pride in this elegant approach. Though watercolors are handsome, they require much experience and are time-consuming to mix. They are also slow to dry. However, when time is pressing or watercolor skills are lacking, color markers offer a ready alternative.

All the exercises in Part Three employ the following techniques:

- When a marker is in hand, every area to which it is to be applied is colored.
- A test sheet is kept at hand to practice patterns and experiment with shading. To this day, I would not consider working without one. Every new fabric is a challenge that requires practice. Errors in judgment are not at all painful on a test sheet, but they certainly become so when they force you to retrace your drawing.
- Makeup is kept to a minimum: perhaps a bit of eye shadow and blush sparingly applied. Just a touch with the corner of your wedge-tipped marker before the flesh tone dries will allow the color to blend. Never "outline" the lips. The lips are a tone with the opening of the mouth accented with a fine line. I use a fine sepia marker for the upper lip and a fine lipstick-color (red, orange, pink) marker for the lower lip. For a glossy look, I try to leave a spot of the paper free of color. If that fails, a dot of white pencil or opaque paint will do.
- If light source and shading are employed in a rendering, the hair is never left to one color. A second tone and often the white of the paper are used to suggest luster.

Floral Print

This example employs the "coloring book" approach (the figure and garment are completely drawn and then colored). It has been rendered flat, without shading or highlights. This technique offers a clean look that works well with nonsheen fabrics. The small floral print on a black background looks more difficult to render than it is. However, the steps outlined below can only be used successfully when the print has a very dark background (black, navy, or bottle green).

To begin, place your guide rough under the page that is to receive the finished work. Trace the figure and garment thoughtfully with a fine black marker. Before applying the skirt pattern to your final drawing, practice it on your test sheet. To color:

1 Apply the flesh tone. Before the face dries, add the blush to the cheeks and it will blend. Now color the sleeveless top and randomly dot the skirt with the same tone. Then color the belt and other accessories of the same color, and begin to randomly dot the skirt.

2 Finish dotting the skirt with the second color, and then apply the third color to the hat and dot the skirt. With a medium-point black marker, loosely enclose the colored dots within ragged circles, suggesting petals. Fill in between the flowers as you go.

3 When the ground is finished, a small dot in the center of each flower will add to the floral look. A tone under the brim of the hat gives dimension. Complete the rendering by ribbing the hat and completing the face.

Plaid

To begin, carefully plan the pattern on your guide rough in pencil first, and then add fine marker over it for greater visibility. Use a square grid to create a large check. First work horizontally, then vertically. The upper and lower parts of the bent arms are treated as individual shapes, as are the columns of fullness in the skirt. The horizontals of the skirt must relate to the hemline, so start from the bottom and work up, making adjustments in placement as you approach the hem of the jacket. The verticals of the skirt taper into gathers and folds. All the squares of the grid on the skirt and the jacket must be the same scale.

When you are satisfied that the figure, garment, pattern, and accessories are in order on your guide rough, place it under your page and trace thoughtfully with a fine black marker. To loosen the look of this rendering, the color has been indicated with some dropouts where the white of the paper shows. This is an option, not a rule. Here, the coloring book approach is used with shading added. This rendering will require practice and color experiments on your test sheet.

1 Apply the base tone to the garment; then do the accessories. While these are drying, color the flesh tone. Add the blush and eye shadow with just a touch of color *before the face dries,* and they will blend nicely. When the garment base tone is dry, shade with a darker tone that tests well on your test sheet. When the shading is dry, start applying the major plaid tone—first horizontals, then verticals.

2 If you are not sure that the horizontals are dry, add the shading to the accessories before starting the verticals. When all is dry, darken the crossover squares with a darker tone or a few more coats of the original tone. To indicate woven texture apply closely placed diagonal lines to the plaid tone with your finest-line black marker.

3 Finish the weave. Now complete the face and shade it. Colored pencils are used for the linear detail of the plaid. (A white line was drawn and then colored red for brightness.)

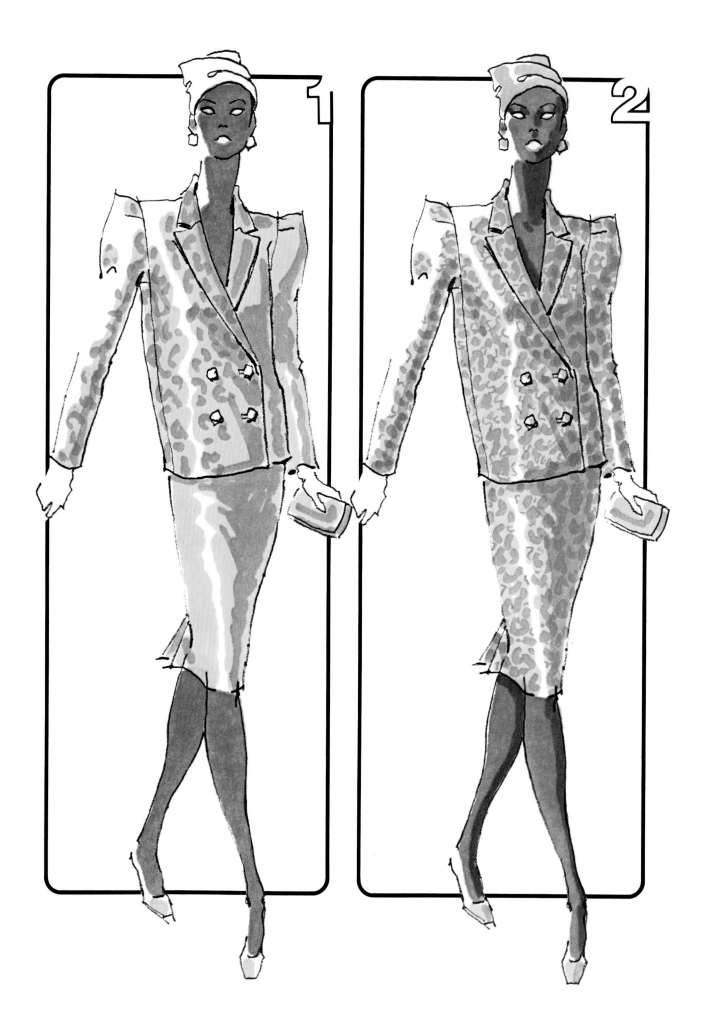

Brocade

This luxurious patterned fabric has been made from a wide variety of materials—silks, rayon, precious metals, and other metallics. Currently, mylar is widely used in brocades because of its light weight.

Brocades come in a great number of patterns, such as floral, paisley, and scroll. The scale of these patterns varies but is commonly bold. The example shown captures the mood more than the specific design and could be swatched in numerous patterns of matching color. Though lustrous, the luster is subtle.

Place your guide rough under the page on which the finished drawing is to be rendered. With a fine black marker, carefully draw the figure and garment. To color:

1 Apply the base tone to the garment, leaving a bit of white paper highlight. Color the face with flesh tone and dot with blush and eye shadow. Complete the flesh tone. When the garment is dry, add the shading. Let dry, and then start the pattern with the second tone. Experiments on your test sheet are definitely in order.

2 Finish the second tone. Apply the base color to the accessories. With a darker flesh tone, shade the face, neck, and legs. Start adding the third tone to the shaded areas only.

3 Finish the third tone. Add colored-pencil pattern on the base color and white-pencil line pattern in the shaded areas. For more contrast, opaque white paint can be used. Complete the face and accessories.

Satin

Though a soft, crepe-backed satin is suggested in this rendering of an evening ensemble, the same approach will work equally well to depict a lustrous silk. The fabric of the bodice has been resurfaced with paillettes (large sequins); the male figure, as you can see, is conventionally attired in a black tuxedo with peaked satin lapels.

We are still employing the coloring book technique with shading. Because of the extreme contrast of highlights and dark shadows, this fabric demands control. Practice first on your test sheet.

Plan a guide rough, place it under the page, and thoughtfully draw the figures with a fine black marker. Note that illustrators often use a darker skin shade for men to convey a more rugged impression. Makeup and finer skin are presumed to lighten the face of a woman.

1 (Female) Apply the flesh tone to the face and neck. Indicate blush and eye shadow before the face dries; then do the leg. Color the first tone on the garments, leaving strong highlights.
  (Male) Apply a darker flesh tone and a base tone to the suit. Save the silk lapels for Step 3.

2 (Female) Apply the base color to the hair. With the darker flesh tone, shade the face, neck, and leg. Apply accents and shading to the garments with the lighter tone of the garment.
  (Male) Apply the base color to the hair. Shade the face and hand with a darker flesh tone. With a black marker, show accents and shading on the suit.

3 (Female) Draw the disks of the paillettes with your finest marker. If more sparkle is desired, use opaque white paint to pick out a small scattering of paillettes from the darkest accents.
  (Male) Shade the shirt sparingly with light gray. Color the lapels medium gray; add black marker before it dries, allowing the black to "bleed" off irregularly near the bottom. When dry, accent the lapels with a fine white pencil line at the edges and down the inside roll.
  (Male, Female) Accent the hair and complete the faces and accessories.

Chiffon

Because the tone of sheer fabrics varies with the number of layers in different parts of the garment, several shades are needed to indicate the darkening effect of the different layers. The following directions will work for most sheers, though they will differ in line quality and silhouette. (For example, chiffon is soft, while organza and net are crisp.) For this exercise, I recommend an alternative technique: *color and accent.* The color is applied first, the linear detail accents last. Practice is vital!

1 With the guide rough in place under the page, apply the flesh tone and blush and eye shadow before the face dries. The underdress is colored next. In this example, areas of the paper are left uncolored to suggest a very high luster fabric. Shade in the flesh.

2 When all the colors are dry, accents and shading in a darker tone are added. The palest tone of the chiffon overdress is applied when all the previous colors are dry. It describes the web and length of the sleeves, the neckline and silhouette of the skirt. Apply the base tone to the hair while the overdress dries. When the palest tone is dry, add another coat to the areas where the fabric is doubled. In this case, the doubled areas are (A) where the sleeves drape under the arms, and (B) where the back of the skirt flares from the underdress (from the waist to the back hemline). If more contrast is desired, let the doubled areas dry and add another coat of color. The underdress tone is now used to indicate the folds of the drapery on the sleeves and bodice. With the same tone, start the overlap of the gathered columns.

3 Finish the overlaps. The marker used to shade the underdress can now be used to accent the gathers and folds over the underdress. Accent the hair with the second tone. Then, with a minimum of fine marker lines, complete the face and hair and apply accents and detail. The hemline should be subtly seen within the folds and around the back of the skirt. Don't overdraw, or the loose feel of this technique will be lost.

Taffeta

Taffeta is a very crisp, lustrous fabric that rustles when in movement. Its gathers, folds, and stress accents are sharp and angular. There is a strong contrast between the highlights and the shaded areas. The rendering technique used for this example is color and accent. The color is applied first, the linear accents and details last.

1 With your guide rough in place, indicate the flesh color and add blush and eye shadow before the face dries. Color the dress with its base tone, leaving some highlights down one side.

2 Apply the base tone to the hair and shade the flesh and accessories. Shade the dress with sharp angular folds and gathers. The stance of the pose and the cut of the garment will suggest where to place stress folds.

3 Finish the face and hair. Add the darkest accents of tone to stress and gather folds. When all is totally dry, use the side of a white pencil point to pick out highlights; for maximum luster, place them at the edge of shaded areas. If the highlights need strengthening, add some opaque white paint. Complete with linear accents, using a fine black marker.

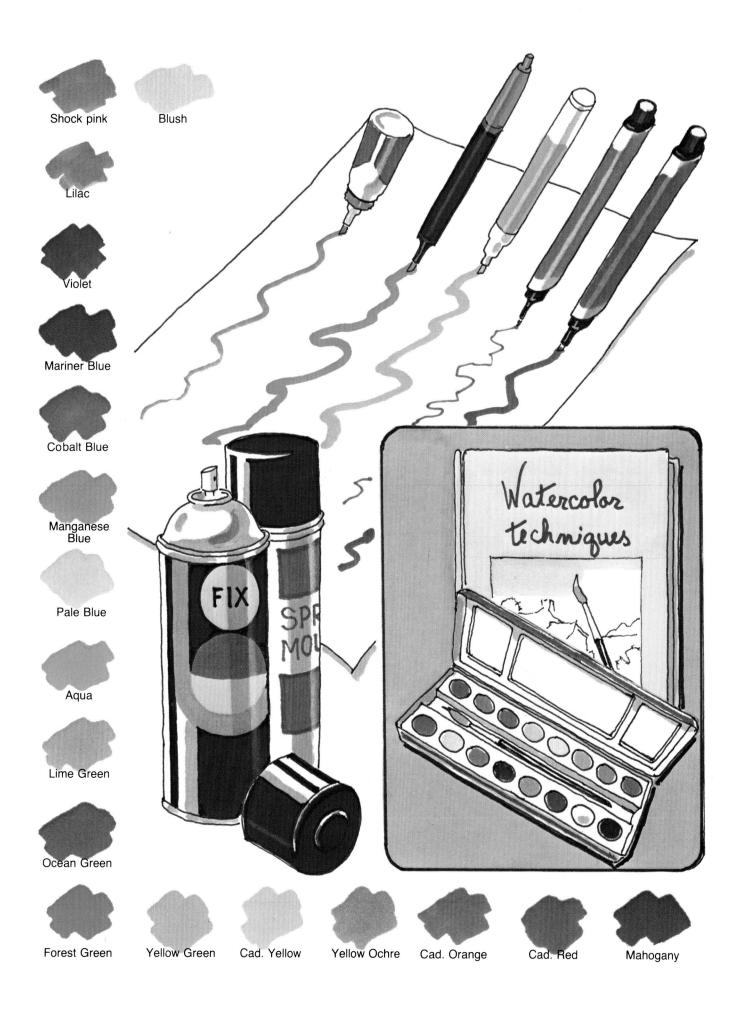

Shock pink

Blush

Lilac

Violet

Mariner Blue

Cobalt Blue

Manganese Blue

Pale Blue

Aqua

Lime Green

Ocean Green

Forest Green

Yellow Green

Cad. Yellow

Yellow Ochre

Cad. Orange

Cad. Red

Mahogany

More Tools
and Materials

The art markers shown here have become a popular medium with designers and illustrators for communicating color and pattern quickly and efficiently. Although not inexpensive, art markers are a versatile and effective tool. Use the chisel point markers to cover large areas and the finer point markers for detail. A suggested starting pallet borders these two pages.

Watercolors, either transparent or opaque, are an elegant but exacting medium. They require specialized training. If they interest you, purchase a good book on the subject or enroll in some watercolor classes.

Other materials shown on these pages include a **spray fixative** to reduce marker bleeding (fuzzing out) and marker fading over time, and **spray mount adhesive** for mounting your drawings. For minor corrections on white paper and for detail or highlights, a water soluble white paint from either a jar or a tube is applied with a medium (#6) or a fine (#3) watercolor brush. Black and white charcoal and colored pencils are useful for accent and detail.

Pads made especially to reduce bleeding in markers are available. Watercolors require their own special paper. Explore your local art goods store for other materials that might attract you. Pastels, colored inks, and colored or textured paper stock offer other options to inspire you.

DARK SEPIA

SUNTAN

BEIGE

NUMBER 3　　**NUMBER 5**　　**NUMBER 7**

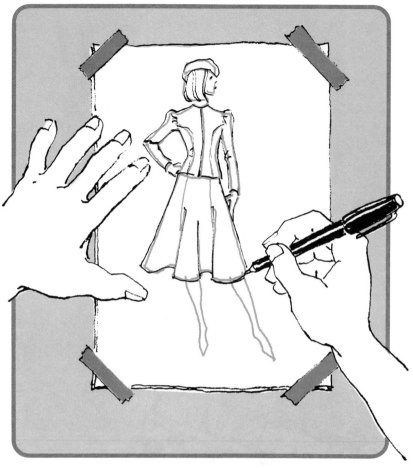

Marker Techniques

Colored markers, once their limitations are understood and, with practice, mastered, are a modern, quick, clean tool for indicating color and pattern.

Markers have a tendency to spread, or "bleed," after application, so always practice on a test sheet of the same type of paper you will be using for your finished rendering. (The marker color and bleed may vary on different paper stock.) This test sheet is also used for experimentation with pattern or texture, required before you can apply either one to your final drawing. Your guide rough may double as a bleed sheet to protect your working surface in case the marker also bleeds through the paper on which you are working.

For practice, draw some shapes on your test sheet and color them to see how close you can get to a line without bleeding over the edge. Markers are not compatible with pencil lines. When the two come in contact, the results are a smudged line, muddy color, and a soiled marker.

Use a chisel-point marker to cover large areas. Fine-point markers used for this purpose will cause streaky overlaps and a blunted point; save them for detail work. Always color complete shapes within the rendering. Use front closures, hems, seams, and folds as guidelines. Never allow a partially colored shape to dry before finishing it. Wet color meeting dry color will create an ugly overlap line.

A darker color may be applied over a lighter tone for shading or pattern. Allow the first tone to dry for a sharp edge. If a softly blended edge is required (such as a blush on the cheeks), the base tone must still be wet. Never apply a lighter color over a darker color. The darker color will be diluted and disfigured.

Choose colors for use with a specific figure or even two figures (one can be drying for the next tone while the other is being colored). Keep other markers out of reach while working to avoid accidentally applying the wrong one to an almost finished work—with certain disappointment! When markers are not in use, keep them firmly capped to avoid drying out and costly replacement.

Two Marker Options

Both of these techniques require that a guide rough of the drawing be completed and used under the working page.

On the facing page:

Top: Trace the garment on the figure and complete all the line work. *Bottom:* Color, accent, and shade. Add texture or pattern of fabric. This technique is not unlike that used in a coloring book.

On this page—for a looser and lighter effect:

Top: Apply the color, shading, and texture or pattern of fabric. *Bottom:* The construction lines and a minimum of accents are all that is needed to complete the look.

Crisp

For a crisp look, the lines should be fine and drawn quickly. Folds and gathers are somewhat angular. The silhouette is full, and the folds at the hemline are sharp.

Soft

The soft look has a slender silhouette. The folds and gathers drape and are softly rounded. The skirt falls in slender columns with softened edges at the hemline.

Line Quality

A look at any pattern book will show that specific fabrics are recommended for each garment. By the hand, weight, and finish of fabrics, the designer can tell the type of construction that can be attempted. For example, it is highly unlikely that the garment used on this page would ever be manufactured in coat-weight flannel; the bulk would be awkward and inappropriate.

The same considerations of hand, weight, and finish confront the illustrator. The fabric suggests the type of line required for drawing the illustration to convey the look of the actual garment as accurately as possible. On pages 138 through 141 are six examples of line-quality possibilities. A discussion under each figure explains the line quality used when these fabrics are drawn.

Hold your pencil very lightly so that you can pivot it easily to create different line weights, as in the drawing below.

On page 141 there is also a list of fabrics appropriate for each line quality.

Bulky

The thickness of the fabric is shown at the neckline and cuffs. Lines are bolder. The silhouette is full, and the folds and gathers are rounded. The edges of the folds at the hemline are blunted.

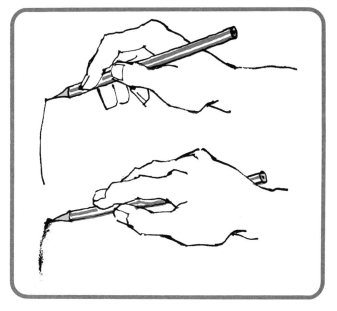

Clinging

The clinging look is a more pronounced version of the soft look. The silhouette may reveal more of the body contours. A clinging garment drapes in very close folds.

Sheer

There is a large variety of sheer looks from soft to very crisp, depending on the specific sheer fabric being illustrated. The silhouette can range from soft and slender to very bouffant. When gathered, the inner columns of fabric show through the outer columns. The sheerness is indicated by showing the fabric color double in these folds and the hemline following both the inner and outer folds.

Line Quality
☐ Clinging-Sheer-Body

A swatch of the fabric in your free hand is a helpful aid when you are illustrating any garment. There is a wide variety of textile weights and finishes possible from the same fibers. This tactile awareness of the hand of the fabric will influence the line quality of your finished drawing.

Examples of Fabric Types

The following fabrics are appropriate for the line qualities shown on pages 138–141.

- *Crisp:* Polished cotton, Chintz, Linen, Taffeta, Organdy
- *Soft:* Challis, Gauze, Crepe, Jersey, Cotton flannel
- *Bulky:* Terrycloth, Camel's hair, Tweed, Corduroy, Vicuna
- *Clinging:* Tricot, Matte jersey, Crepe-back satin (Bias Cut), Silk (Bias Cut), Panné velvet
- *Sheer:* Chiffon, Organza, Voile, Tulle, Lace
- *Body:* Pique, Poplin, Peau de soie, Brocade, Faille

Body

A fabric with body is related to a crisp fabric, but it is heavier. It sometimes has a pile, but stops short of bulky. Any fullness will stand away from the body in silhouette. The lines are bold, and the folds are slightly angular.

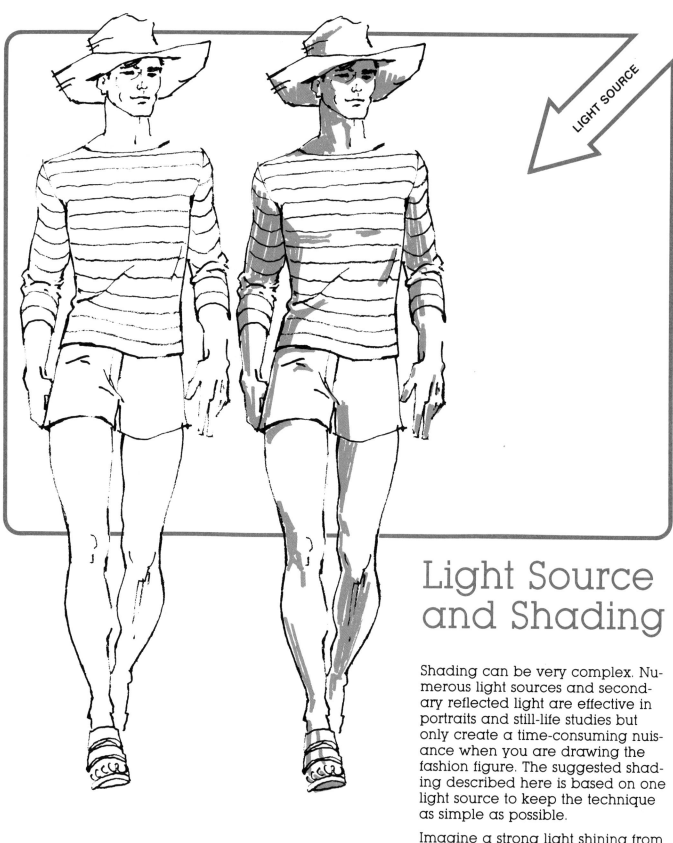

Light Source and Shading

Shading can be very complex. Numerous light sources and secondary reflected light are effective in portraits and still-life studies but only create a time-consuming nuisance when you are drawing the fashion figure. The suggested shading described here is based on one light source to keep the technique as simple as possible.

Imagine a strong light shining from above and from one side or the other onto the figure (arrow). The shading will then occur on the figure much as it does on the sphere, as illustrated. Compare the two figures on this page. They illustrate the added volume and movement

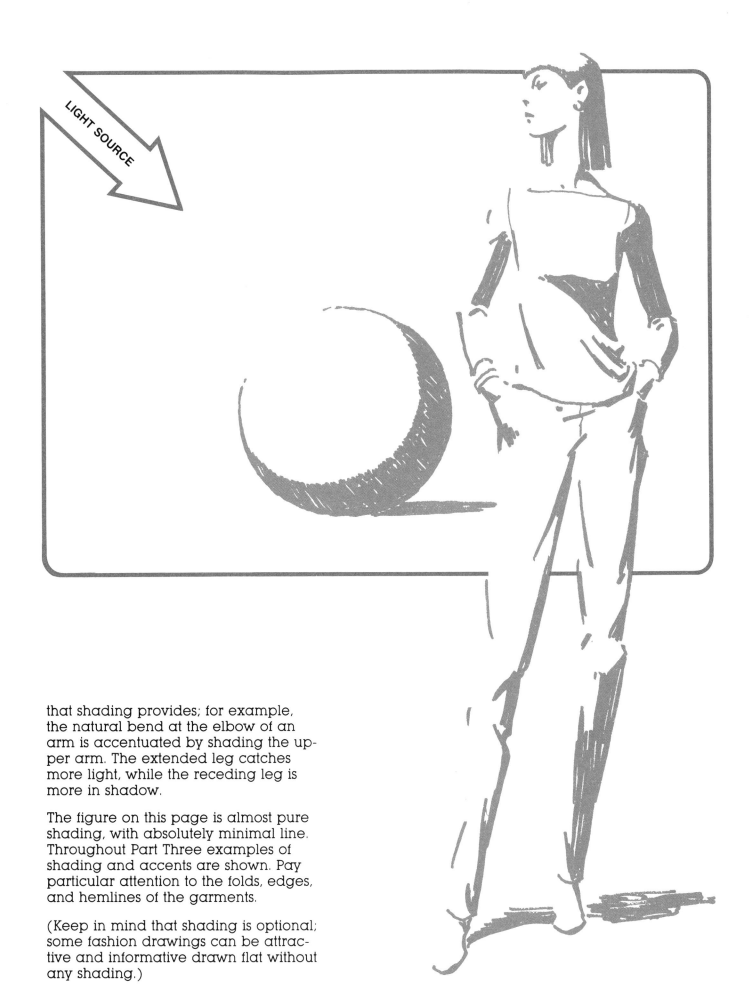

that shading provides; for example, the natural bend at the elbow of an arm is accentuated by shading the upper arm. The extended leg catches more light, while the receding leg is more in shadow.

The figure on this page is almost pure shading, with absolutely minimal line. Throughout Part Three examples of shading and accents are shown. Pay particular attention to the folds, edges, and hemlines of the garments.

(Keep in mind that shading is optional; some fashion drawings can be attractive and informative drawn flat without any shading.)

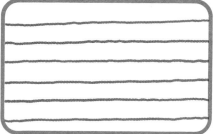

VERTICAL

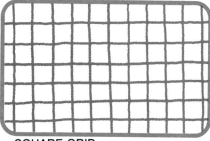

HORIZONTAL

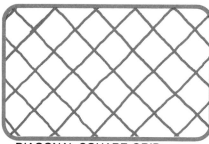

SQUARE GRID

Planning Pattern

Pattern is created by a repetition of lines or shapes. Learning to control these components when applying them to a drawing takes concentration and much practice. Not only must the pattern "repeat" be consistent, but the contour of the body, as well as folds, gathers, and the cut of the garment, must be considered.

The first skill to acquire is how to draw stripes. Vertically, they form a pattern. Horizontal stripes are another basic pattern. Combined, the two create a network, or grid, upon which most other patterns are based. It is used as a guideline for checks, plaids, and the repeat of motifs or shapes. The grid may be staggered either horizontally to form the brick grid or vertically to form the half-drop grid. Put the grid on the diagonal, or bias, and another group of pattern bases is formed. Stretch the bias grid from squares to diamonds and more possibilities are apparent.

Samples of all the grids described above and examples of their uses in fabric pattern are illustrated on these pages. Practice them over and over on a test paper before applying them to a garment. The exercises on drawing pattern that begin on page 148 are designed to be drawn over a croquis figure or a rough draft of the garment. It may be necessary to trace a number of drafts of the patterned garment before the results are satisfactory. If the finished drawing is to be on a paper or board that is too opaque for tracing, the pattern

DIAGONAL SQUARE GRID

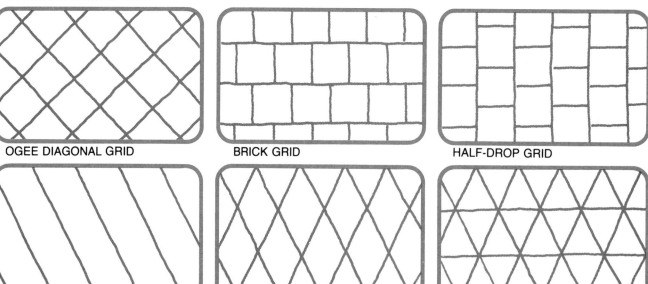

OGEE DIAGONAL GRID

BRICK GRID

HALF-DROP GRID

DIAGONAL

DIAMOND GRID

TRIANGLE GRID

can be very lightly planned. When the drawing is complete, the guidelines that have not been absorbed can be carefully erased.

- *Vertical stripes:* In this example the guidelines are broadened to form the stripe. The alternating colors add interest.
- *Horizontal stripes:* This stripe is created by coloring between alternate pairs of guidelines.
- *Checks:* Color lightly between alternate guidelines both vertically and horizontally. The crossovers, or intersections, are accented with the full strength of the color.
- *Polka dots:* The dots must be organized on a diagonal grid. If not, they become a different pattern—random dots.
- *Ogee:* This pattern is also organized on a diagonal grid. Be careful to match the curved, onion-like shapes.
- *Geometric print:* In this pattern, organized on a brick grid, each brick is divided diagonally with a circle in the center.
- *Floral print:* Organized on a half-drop grid, this **motif** (dominant recurring visual element) alternates direction as it repeats vertically.
- *Diagonal stripes:* This is a diagonal repetition.
- *Argyle:* This pattern is organized on the diamond grid in alternating tones. A secondary dotted grid bisects the diamond pattern.
- *Triangular print:* The triangular grid is used for the alternating and staggered motif.

VERTICAL STRIPES

HORIZONTAL STRIPES

CHECKS

POLKA DOTS

FLORAL PRINT

GEOMETRIC PRINT

OGEE

TRIANGULAR PRINT

ARGYLE

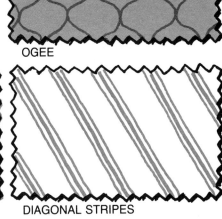

DIAGONAL STRIPES

Scaling the Pattern

When you are drawing pattern or texture for fashion purposes, you are trying to give the general effect or "look" of a fabric. There is no need to reproduce it in minute detail. Begin by studying and handling a sample swatch, yardage, or a garment itself until you are familiar with its strongest features. Then walk away from the fabric. View it at the distance you would be viewing a full human figure clothed in it. (A distance of 3 or 4 feet will do.) Suggest the appearance of the fabric from this normal viewing distance. You will discover that much less detail is visible than can be observed in the close-up range.

When you are working from a swatch, an excellent aid is to pin it to any finished garment available. Place the garment with the affixed swatch so that the entire garment is in view. You can then observe how the pattern on the swatch relates to the host garment and determine the proper scale. It is tempting to work with the fabric right under your nose. Don't yield! The scale will grow, become overdetailed, take more time, and fail to convey the effect of the pattern.

Indicating
the Pattern

Patterns are shown on the fashion drawing to communicate to the viewer where they will occur on the garment. To create a light touch, or even to save time, fashion designers and illustrators will sometimes *indicate* the pattern, texture, and even the color, rather than complete them on the entire garment. Though this technique may appear easier, it takes practice and skill. Too much indication may lose the effect. Too little may fail to offer enough information. If the indications are too spotty or vague, they might suggest an occasional motif or a very widely spaced repeat pattern, and thus totally confuse the viewer.

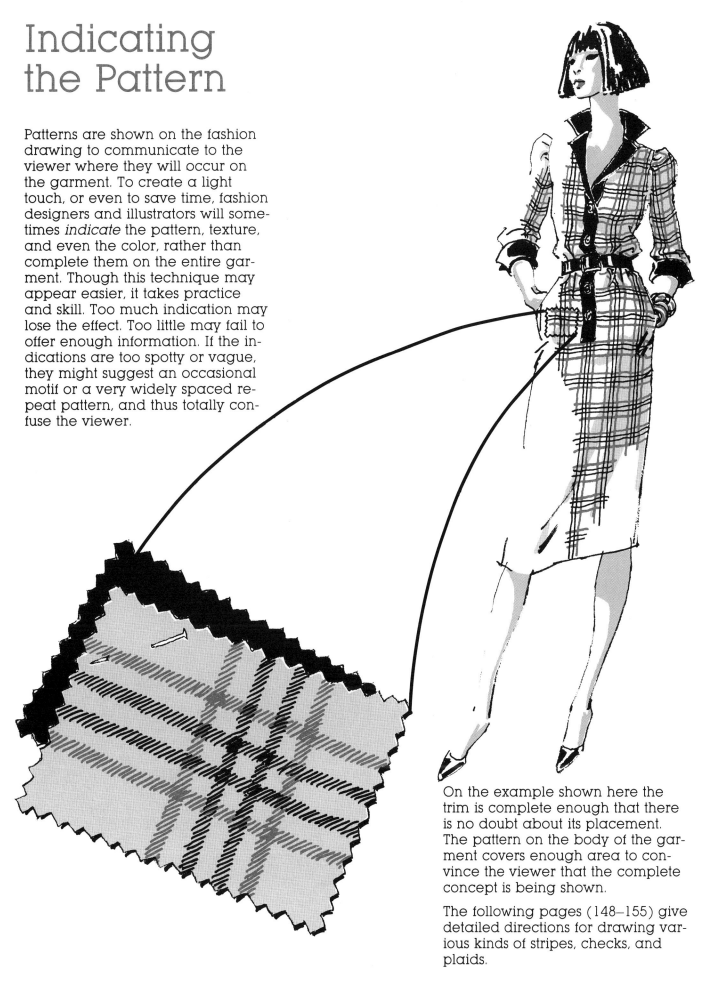

On the example shown here the trim is complete enough that there is no doubt about its placement. The pattern on the body of the garment covers enough area to convince the viewer that the complete concept is being shown.

The following pages (148–155) give detailed directions for drawing various kinds of stripes, checks, and plaids.

Stripes

Vertical

1 On the croquis, draw the guideline for the first stripe down the torso centerline on the garment. Draw a guideline down the center of the sleeve shape. Next, draw evenly spaced guidelines to the left. Note the arrows. Be sure they maintain their spacing from top to bottom. Make adjustments for body contours and gathers or folds.

2 Draw guidelines to the right of the torso centerline. Draw guidelines on the remaining sleeve. Using the same method as above, draw guidelines on the skirt.

3 With the guidelines complete, put your croquis under the paper on which you intend to complete your drawing. Apply shading and draw finished stripes according to the fabric being rendered.

Horizontal

1 Draw a guideline describing the contour of the bust. Next, draw guidelines upward, adjusting to the contour of the body. Keep the lines evenly spaced according to the stripes to be rendered.

2 Work down from the bust guideline. Adjust to the body contour and end up matching the hem. The last stripe must relate to the hemline. The guidelines on the sleeves should work down from the shoulders and relate to the stripes on the body of the garment at the arm's eye. For the lower arm, work up from the wrists to the elbow folds. The stripes should curve with the opposing contours of the upper and lower arm. The folds at the bend of the elbow will mask any spacing problems. If the arm is not bent, work from the shoulder and plan carefully.

3 With the guidelines complete, the finished stripes—broad, narrow, or a combination of both—can be rendered accurately.

Checks

The following technique applies to any basic check, from a small gingham check to a large, overscale novelty check. The diagonal weave lines in Step 3 are drawn only if they are apparent on the swatch at a full-length distance. The darker tone of the intersections establishes the color of the check.

1 Combining the directions for vertical and horizontal stripes, lightly draw a grid on the garment. Space the lines to form squares indicating the scale of the pattern you are rendering.

2 Apply a medium tone of the desired color of the finished check between alternate pairs of grid guidelines. Start coloring the squares with the full color tone at the intersections of the broad stripes.

3 Complete the checks with the full-tone intersections. Apply ground color and shading, if desired.

Plaid

1 Establish a grid of squares as above, carefully scaled to the pattern of your swatch. While planning the grid, adjust for body contours and folds. On the sample garment shown, the grid on the pockets (and sometimes on the front-closure placket) is usually on the bias (diagonal).

2 Add the secondary lines on either side of the lines of the initial grid. Keep the spacing consistent.

3 With the planning complete, the final color or tone is applied. Finish with buttons, physical details, and accents.

Windowpane

This pattern is based on a check but is more widely spaced with finer lines.

1 Lightly draw the grid to the proper scale, with attention to the body contours and garment folds.

2 With the grid as a guide apply the lighter color or tone. A small square of the darker shade of color or tone is placed on each intersection.

3 Complete the drawing with garment details, physical details, and accents.

Tattersall

This pattern is like a double windowpane in two colors.

1 Lightly draw the primary grid. Then draw the secondary grid.

2 With two colors or two tones finish each grid.

3 Complete the drawing with garment details, physical details, and accents.

Herringbone

The herringbone pattern is derived from the weave of the textile. It can range from small, fine diagonal lines on a flat fabric to strong, bold lines on a bulky textured fabric. Before adding the diagonal lines to your drawing, establish a rhythm on your test sheet to insure consistency in spacing and thickness of line.

1 Lightly draw with pencil vertical guidelines on the garment body and sleeves. Apply shading. Note the guidelines on the lapel and sleeves relate to the cut of the garment and folds.

2 Using a fine marker, start to draw fine diagonal lines between the guidelines, one column at a time. These diagonals alternate directions from row to row. The strokes do not have to join at the guidelines.

3 Add dark accents to garment. Then complete diagonals and remove guidelines. Complete drawing with features and accessory details.

Houndstooth

The houndstooth pattern is derived from the diagonal weave of the textile. Although it is a diagonal weave, it appears to be a checked pattern with "teeth" connecting the squares. The scaling can range from a tiny conservative check to an extra large novelty one.

1 Lightly draw with pencil a square grid on garment. Apply shading. With a fine-tip marker, cover each intersection with a carefully scaled solid square box.

2 Link the squares in each vertical row by drawing a fine line from the lower corner of one to the upper corner of its neighbor. To complete the pattern, draw a diagonal line through each box at the same angle as those linking the boxes.

3 When the drawing is dry, remove guidelines with kneaded eraser. Add accents and complete features and accessories.

Diagonal Stripes

1 Establish the angle required by lightly drawing a diagonal guideline across the garment—in this case, from the shoulder to the hip. Next, work upward and to the left with evenly spaced lines, adjusting their contour to the body.

2 Work downward and to the right, keeping the lines evenly spaced. Use the same technique described above to indicate the stripes of the skirt. Make adjustments for any tucks, folds, or gathers that may be encountered.

3 With the guidelines in place, the final rendering can be completed.

Polka Dots

1 Using "diagonal stripes" technique, lightly draw a grid on the garment. Scale it to the fabric and garment being rendered. The lines of the grid must be at right angles to form squares. If elongated diamond shapes occur, the grid won't work for polka dots.

2 At each point where the lines of the grid cross, place a carefully drawn polka dot. Be sure they are all the same size. Make adjustments for any tucks or folds.

3 Remove the grid lines, and the polka dots alone become the pattern.

Floral Prints

A large-scale floral print such as the one on the dress illustrated here is less demanding than the tightly controlled patterns shown previously.

1 Apply shading. Use the intersections of a large diagonal grid to indicate placement of the most prominent motif. When all the motifs are in place, start coloring them.

2 Complete primary motifs and add on the secondary ones. Then add darker tones to flower centers and leaves.

3 Finish by adding accents, features, and accessories.

Geometric Prints

1 Apply shading. Use the techniques for planning both horizontal and diagonal stripes to create a grid on the garment. Do the horizontals first and then the steep diagonals crossing at the horizontals. The resulting triangle pattern can now be colored. Start coloring the triangles that point *up*ward.

2 When these triangles have been colored, start adding the linear triangle detail to the triangles that point *down*ward. Add a small triangle pointing upward inside the previously colored one.

3 Finish the linear triangle detail. Complete the drawing with features, accents, and accessories.

Planning Texture

Texture refers to the visual or tactile surface characteristics and appearance of a fabric. Whether large or small, all textures cast a shadow. The depth of the shadow increases with the depth of the texture. Learning to control texture requires careful scaling and a lot of practice—be careful not to overdo texture or it will look like a pattern.

Let's begin with the very popular texture that is a result of quilting. **Quilting** is made by firmly stitching together two layers of cloth with some soft padding between them. The stitching can be in straight lines, crossing lines, or ornamental patterns. Three major kinds of quilting are shown here and on the next page: tunnel, diagonal, and ogee. In all three cases, the silhouette is bulky and the edges are rounded.

Tunnel Quilting

Tunnel quilting, which may run horizontally or vertically, is usually used on outerwear. It is drawn with a bulky silhouette and rounded edges.

1 Draw the seams of the quilting with your finest line. In this case the stitching is in vertical, evenly spaced columns. The collar, cuffs, and hem are where the silhouette is most affected by the puffy filling and the sewn quilting lines. Note the roundness of the hem at the base of each column.

2 Shade lightly along one side of each column. Add dark accents at collar, cuffs, and front closure and on the edge of the garment away from the light source. Begin adding irregular puckers along the quilting seams.

3 Finish the drawing by adding buttons and accessories.

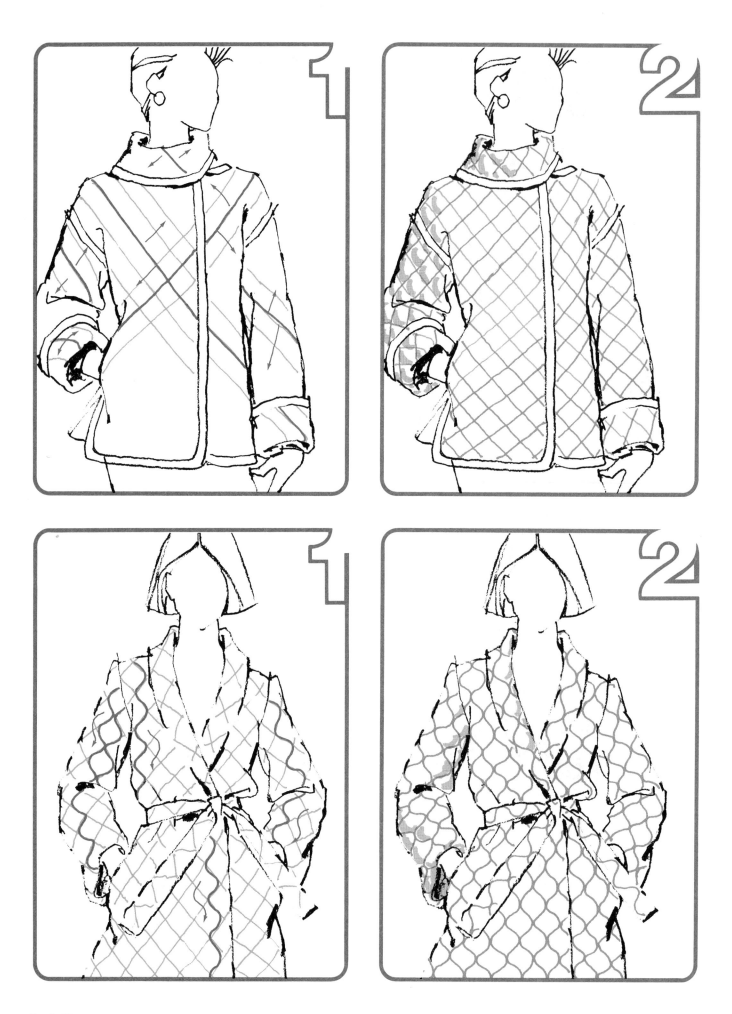

Diagonal Quilting

Diagonal quilting is often used for various types of jackets. This garment combines texture and a complex pattern to present a greater challenge than tunnel quilting.

1 Lightly establish a diagonal grid, keeping in mind body contours, garment construction, and folds.

2 Complete the grid. With a specific light source in mind, begin to draw crescent strokes on the padding between the stitching. These strokes can be drawn on the entire garment, or for a lighter effect, they can occur only where shading would be added.

3 Adjust the silhouette of the garment to suggest the puffiness of the padding. Add a light tone for shading and some dark accents. Draw details, features, and accessories to complete the drawing.

Ogee Quilting

Ogee quilting is often used for robes. It is the most challenging kind of quilting to draw because of the complex shadows cast by this texture.

1 Lightly draw the diagonal grid. Using the grid as a guide, draw S-shaped curved lines meeting at each apex.

2 Finish the ogee pattern and start adding crescent shading. It is difficult to keep the shapes between the stitching consistent, so much practice is required on a test sheet before attempting the final drawing.

3 Adjust the silhouette as above and add accents and details to complete the drawing.

Smocking

Smocking is a process in which the fabric is stitched into very small puff-pleats or gathers, forming a three-dimensional honeycomb pattern.

1 Lightly draw a diamond grid on the bodice using the diagonal stripes technique.

2 Add shading to suggest dimension. Begin to add pairs of slightly curved linear accents connecting the intersections to indicate the fullness of the puckered fabric.

3 Finish the accents and complete the drawing with features and accessories.

Shirring

Shirring is constructed by closely spaced parallel rows of gathers. The shirring in this example is elasticized.

1 Starting at the waist, lightly draw closely spaced horizontal lines around the torso. Use a slightly jagged line to suggest the rows of stitching.'

2 Apply shading and start to add short, irregular strokes to indicate the gathers between the stitching.

3 Finish gathers and add accents and features.

Slubs

Linens and raw silk are excellent examples of fabrics with an irregular slub texture. The silhouette is usually crisp. The texture is caused by irregularities in the weave of the fabric, which in light colors causes shadows and in dark colors catches the light. The slub texture can occur in either horizontal or vertical directions or both. As in drawing other textures, you should give scattered indication of effect, to avoid the appearance of pattern.

1 On light colored fabric begin by adding shading. On dark fabric start by coloring with a medium tone.

2 Begin to draw the slub texture on the light fabric with quick, irregular dashes and a very fine line. On the dark fabric add the shading with a dark toned marker.

3 Finish the details and accessories on both figures. On the dark fabric use a white pencil to indicate the slub.

Seersucker

Classic seersucker is a crisp summer-weight fabric with a linear texture of puckers.

1 Using the vertical stripes technique, lightly plan closely spaced guidelines. Apply shading.

2 With your fine-point marker, apply slightly shaky lines to suggest the puckered texture.

3 Finish drawing with features and accessories.

Corduroy

Corduroy is a pile fabric with a linear texture known as the **wale.** The widths of wale range from the softest infant-wear pinwale to the very bulky wide-wale and novelties. This example is a mid-wale cord usually used for sportswear. In this technique the texture is applied only on the shaded portion of the garment to avoid making it look like stripes. Pay special attention to where the light tone is applied.

1 Apply shading. Plan diamond grid for argyle sweater; fill in lighter tone diamonds.

2 Indicate the texture of the wales with closely spaced fine lines starting just outside the tone areas. Fill in the darker tone in alternate diamonds of argyle. Add ribbing to sweater.

3 Draw top stitching on lapel, front closure, and pockets. Complete drawing by adding accents, facial features, accessories, and dotted line detail in argyle.

Eyelet

Eyelet is a mechanically applied embroidery with perforations. Because of the process involved in feeding the fabric into the machine, a crisp fabric with some body is usually used. A characteristic of most eyelets is an embroidered scalloped border. There are many variations of motifs and placement. The example shown is typical.

1 Lightly draw a grid of evenly spaced diagonal lines on garment to plan the spacing of the pattern. Do one section of garment at a time. Start drawing the scalloped border with a double line to indicate the embroidered edge.

2 Finish grid and scallops. Start drawing the floral motif centered in each scallop. Draw the three tiny perforations in clusters at each intersection of the grid.

3 Complete drawing with accents. Note the dropout of pattern as a highlight to indicate a white or pastel fabric.

Lace

Lace, a delicate openwork fabric, varies from soft to crisp. Most laces feature a floral or scroll motif; many have a scalloped edge with a hairline fringe and a floral motif centered in each scallop. Lace is used as a trim in many ways, but when used for a complete garment, lace is usually lined because it is extremely sheer.

1 Draw the silhouette and folds of both garments with delicate double lines and scalloped edges.

Dark dress: Color the lining with a dark-toned marker, being sure to reserve your darkest tone for the shading (in Step 2).

Light dress: Add the shading with a medium tone.

2 *Dark dress:* Add dark shading on the lining with darkest tone. With a fine-point dark marker, render the scalloped edges. Add floral motifs, and connect with a network of fine curved lines.

Light dress: Start indicating floral motifs and cross-hatching with opaque white on the shading.

3 *Both dresses:* Finish the lace details. With a fine-point dark marker, add accents to floral motifs, gathers, and scalloped edge of hemline. Finish with facial features and accessories.

Velvet

Velvet is a soft pile fabric with deep shadows and a medium luster. Edges and seams are highlighted. Velveteen is less lustrous and has more body. This example is accessorized with a heavy lace at collar and cuffs.

1 Draw the garment with a soft silhouette and a hint of bulk indicated by curved edges. Color the garment with a medium-toned marker. Draw cross-hatching of lace with finest-point marker.

2 Add deep shadows with a darker-toned marker. Draw the scalloped edge of the lace with hairline fringe detail. Indicate the gathers and the floral motif within each scallop.

3 Use the broad side of a soft white pencil to suggest fabric luster. Use the pencil point to pick out the highlights along the seams and edges. Add finishing details and accents.

Another option when rendering pile fabrics such as velvets and velours is to use the broad side of a soft leaded pencil to tone and accent the garment. Blend toward the highlights, allowing some paper to show through. Spray with a fixative.

Fur

Lynx

A very bulky silhouette is required as lynx is quite long-haired, though soft and fluffy. The animal's coat is subtly marked and somewhat spotted. This example shows vertical pelts on the body of the garment and horizontal pelts on the sleeves.

1 On the very bulky silhouette draw light lines to indicate where the pelts are sewn together. Lightly shade the edges of the pelts. For the examples shown on this page, the side of a very soft or charcoal pencil point is used for shading.

2 With quick, fine strokes, indicate the length of the fur on the silhouette of the coat. Loosely indicate the animal's markings with flecks.

3 Complete the markings and finish as shown by adding facial features and accessories. This technique will also work for fox, if the spots are eliminated.

Sable

As above, this example is constructed with vertical pelts on the body of the coat and horizontal pelts on the sleeves. Using narrower pelts and slightly less bulk, the following technique will also work for mink.

1 Draw light lines to indicate where the pelts are joined on the bulky silhouette. Shade lightly to blunt the edges of the collar, cuffs, hemline, and the pelt lines.

2 With a darker tone start showing the soft markings down the center of each pelt. The white of the page showing through will serve where highlights are desired. Add accents as you progress. With the side of your pencil, blur the edges of the silhouette to avoid a hard line.

3 Sparingly add some fine hair lines to the silhouette of the coat. Complete the drawing with facial features.

Presentation Skills

Mounting

Mounting reinforces the drawing and allows thumb space for careless viewers.

With a sharp blade, trim mounting board to accommodate the drawing. The top and side margins should match and the bottom margin should be a bit more generous. Using your drawing and a metal-edged ruler as a guide, mark the corners for placement. Place the drawing face down on a large, clean sheet of newsprint. Apply rubber cement, brushing out from the center and onto the newsprint to assure coverage on the edges. Alternatively, apply an aerosol spray mount in a circular motion from top to bottom. Carefully position top corners and smooth the drawing downward.

Matting

Matting offers a more finished look and more protection. However, it requires much practice to achieve a cleanly cut mat. Precut mats may be bought at an art goods store.

Trim mat board to same size as your mounting board. Measure for margins as above, but make a "window" ¼" smaller all the way around. Align mat face down along top edge of mounted drawing. Join with a hinge of masking tape. Fold mat down over mounted drawing. For added protection a sheet of tissue is taped along top edge of the back of your matted drawing, and folded over to protect it during transit. It is folded back for viewing.

The Portfolio

To further protect your drawings and to aid in making an organized presentation, a proper container is required. The least expensive is the *student art portfolio*. It is in black leatherette-covered chipboard with three tie strings. The most expensive is the zipper presentation album with acetate sheet protectors. Clear acetate refill pages are available for this model. A handy size would be 14" x 18" or 17" x 22", depending on the size of your mounted drawings. To keep your portfolio from becoming too heavy, use a lightweight board for mounting. Remember, the portfolio will double in size when opened. If it is too large, your presentation will be awkward and taxing to the viewer.

Your portfolio should contain fashion drawings only. They should relate to the type of apparel produced by the firm to which you are applying. For example, avoid showing ball gowns to a firm that specializes in tailored sportswear. Research the firm by checking their merchandise offerings in department stores, and adjust the concepts in your portfolio accordingly. Twelve to sixteen relevant examples should show your potential. Include both figure and flat working drawings to display your versatility. One figure per page is best, unless showing coordinates of the same fabric mix. Swatch the drawings whenever possible. Finally, be sure to keep your presentation organized, neat, and clean.

Glossary

Accents Emphatic dark shadows.
Accordion pleats Uniform, fanlike pleats repeated to form a relatively full skirt.
A-line skirt Slightly flared skirt darted from the waist for smooth fit over the hip.
Annie Hall Look Eclectic style of feminine dressing favored by actress Diane Keaton's character in the Woody Allen film popular around 1977.
Arm's eye Round hole where sleeve fits body of garment.
Asymmetrical collar A collar that is different on each side of the garment.
Bateau (Boat) neckline Wide, slightly scooped neckline following the collarbone; often matching front and back.
Bias cut Cut diagonally across the grain of the fabric so that any fullness will fall gracefully.
Bishop sleeves Long, full sleeves, usually gathered on a wristband and adopted from a bishop's robe.
Bolero jacket Short, fitted jacket.
Box pleat Made by forming two folded edges, one facing right and the other left. Each box pleat has an inverted pleat on its reverse. (*See also* Inverted pleat.)
Brocade A luxurious patterned fabric with raised design, made from silk, rayon, precious metals and other metallics, and, currently, mylar.
Cap sleeves Usually cut as part of the bodice covering the shoulders only, unless overscale.
Capri pants Very tight, leg-hugging pant that ends just above the ankle. Small slit detail common at hemline. Also known as toreador pants.
Cardigan jacket Collarless front-closure jacket most commonly "V" necked.
Centerline Vertical (plumb) line defining the center of the fashion figure.
Chanel suit Timeless classic, first created by Coco Chanel in 1927. Identified by hip length box jacket with braid trim and pocket detail.
Check Vertical and horizontal bands of color arranged on a square grid. Color intensifies at each intersection.
Chemise Started as an undergarment (as did the shift). As a dress it hangs straight from the shoulders to the hem, with no waistline.
Chiffon A sheer fabric, especially of silk.
Corduroy A pile fabric with a linear texture known as wale.
Cowl neckline Draped neck treatment modeled after a hooded garment—the cowl—formerly worn by monks.
Croquis (kro-*key*) Guide figure to trace over. Originally meant a quick, rough sketch.
Culottes Divided skirt characterized by gathers of fullness or pleats that disguise the division into legs and suggest a conventional skirt.
Cylindrical perspective Representation of a cylindrical shape to convey an impression of three-dimensional space.
Darts Wedge-shaped tucks stitched out of garments to contour them closely to the body.
Destination A point on a garment or figure to which the illustrator chooses to draw.
Dirndl Straight skirt with fullness created by gathers from the waistband.
Divided skirt Skirt divided into two pant legs. (*See also* gaucho pants, culottes).

Dolman sleeve Batwing-shaped sleeve.
Draped neckline Bias-cut fabric manipulated to form draped folds describing the neckline.
Drop-out Places where color has not been applied.
Dropped shoulder Attaching the sleeve well below the shoulder.
Empire The skirt falls from just below the bust. Borrowed from the ancient Romans by the French in Napoleonic times.
Engineered pleats Pleats added for detail.
Eyelet Mechanically applied embroidery with perforations.
Flounce Gathered or bias-cut extension of a garment attached to the hemline.
Flounced skirt Layers of overlapping flounces attached to a foundation under skirt.
Format The size and shape of the sheet of paper on which you are drawing.
Foreshortening Contraction in the direction of depth to suggest projection in space.
Freelance To be employed by more than one firm for individual projects.
Garment construction lines Seams, bust, and other darts, gathers, tucks.
Gathered skirt Full skirt gathered at waistband.
Gaucho pants Simple mid-calf length divided skirt originally worn by Argentine cowboys.
Gored-and-gathered skirt Graceful skirt with both gores and gathers of maximum fullness.
Gored skirt Cut and sewn from flaring shapes to fit smoothly from the waistband with columns of fullness falling from hips.
Grid A network of vertical and horizontal or diagonal lines upon which patterns of most fabrics are based.
Hand The crispness or softness of a garment's fabrication.
Herringbone A pattern derived from the weave of the textiles made up of rows of parallel lines which slope in opposite directions in adjacent rows.
Highlight Bright spot reflecting light.
Hobble skirt Tight, long skirt difficult to walk in, popular around 1912.
Houndstooth A small broken-check textile pattern derived from the diagonal weave of the textile.
Inverted pleat Backward pleat facing inside of garment.
Jewel neckline Plain, round neckline at the base of the throat.
Jodhpurs Full riding breeches, but closely fitted to the leg from just above the knee to the ankle. Brought to the west from India by the British.
Jumpsuit Top and trousers in one piece. Patterned after protective clothing worn by mechanics and painters. Named for garb worn by parachutists in World War Two.
Kimono sleeves Full, wide, long sleeve usually cut in one piece with the bodice, but sometimes set in at a dropped shoulder line. (*See also* Dropped shoulder.)
Knickers Pants gathered on a close fitting band just below the knee.
Knife pleat A relatively wide pleat folding on itself in one direction.
Lace A delicate openwork fabric usually featuring a floral motif and woven from a wide variety of thread weights. It is also a popular trim.
Line quality The appropriate drawing line to render different fabric textures.
Look A total fashion concept reflected by the design, fabrications, and accessories.
Mandarin collar Stand-up slit band.

Middy   A loose overblouse with a sailor collar. (*See also* Sailor collar.)

Miniskirt   Mid-thigh length skirt popular around 1967.

Mono-bust Line   A pushed-up look giving a shelf-like appearance to the breasts. This style became fashionable in the 1880s and continued after the turn of the century.

Motif   A dominant recurrent visual element.

New Look   Silhouette created by Dior in 1947 featuring sloped shoulders; tiny waist; padded hips; full, long skirt.

Ogee   A pattern of curved onionlike shapes.

Pantsuit   Suit style featuring pants and jacket that became popular around 1972.

Pattern   Created by the repetition of lines or shapes.

Pegged pants   Full pantlegs tapered to a close-fitting hemline.

Peplum   A flounce from waist to hips.

Perspective   The art of representing space relationships as they appear to the eye.

Peter Pan collar   Small and round.

Plaid   Variation on the check, introducing more colors and linear detail.

Plumb line   A vertical line for planning the figure on the page.

Polka dots   Identical dots arranged on a diagonal square grid.

Princess line   A vertical seam originating from either the shoulder or the arm's eye to accommodate the bust and indicate the waistline; ends at the hemline.

Proportion   The relationship of the size of the parts to each other and to the size of the whole.

Quilting   The firm stitching together of two layers of cloth with some soft padding between them.

Raglan sleeves   Extending from the neckline and having slanted seams from the underarm to the neck in front and back.

Roll   Opening shape of collar.

Sailor collar   Broad, with a square flap across the back, tapering to a V in front. Often work with a tie found on a middy. (*See also* Middy.)

Satin   A fabric in satin weave, that is, with a lustrous front and dull back.

Scale (*v*)   To regulate or adjust according to a designated ratio; (*n*) the ratio of adjustment chosen; also, the relationship of size of representation to actual object being drawn. *Scaling the figure to the pose.* Picking a figure size that fills the page pleasingly.

Scoop neckline   Rounded, low-cut neckline.

Seersucker   A crisp summerweight fabric with a linear texture of puckers.

Separates   Outfits that combine jackets with skirts or pants.

Set-in sleeves   Stitched into an armhole cut in the front and back sections of a garment.

Shift   A shorter version of the chemise dress, skimming closer to the body.

Shirring   Construction of closely spaced parallel rows of gathers.

Shirtwaist   Tailored blouse or dress with a shirtlike bodice.

Silhouette   Fashion shape.

Slub   Irregular texture caused by irregularities in the weave of the fabric.

Smocking   Process in which fabric is stitched into very small puff-pleats or gathers, forming a three-dimensional honeycomb pattern.

Spray fixative   A spray that reduces marker bleeding and fading.

Spray mount adhesive   A glue to mount drawings.

Sweetheart neckline   High in back, low in front, where it is scalloped to resemble the top of a heart.

Symmetrical collar   The same on both sides of the garment.

Taffeta   A very crisp, lustrous fabric that rustles in movement.

Tattersall   A pattern like a double windowpane in two colors.

Texture   The visual or tactile surface characteristics and appearance of a fabric.

Tier   Gathered skirt layer sewn to the ones above and below.

Tiered skirt   Layered, gathered skirt in which the horizontal layers or tiers are sewn to each other.

Tie-wrap suit   Jacket with no front closure other than the belt.

Top   A separate word usually describing a slipover, back closure, or tunic-type upper garment.

Top stitching   Fine line of visible stitching.

Trapeze influence   1962 look, fitted in front and eased in back to fall full from shoulders.

Tunic   A more or less knee-length upper garment; borrowed from ancient Rome.

Turtleneck   High, close-fitting turn-over collar.

Unpressed pleats   Structured from the waistline to relax into a loose hemline. Rounded folds rather than sharp ones.

Velvet   A closely woven fabric with a pile finish on one side. Lustrous if woven from silk or rayon.

Venting; vents   Opening at the bottom of seam in back of blazer or other jacket.

Vignette   Partial drawing.

Wale   The linear texture of corduroy.

Windowpane   A pattern based on checks but with more widely spaced and finer lines.

Wing Sleeves   Short, flared, gathered at the shoulders.

Yoke   A horizontal division in a garment.

Index